Thompson-Pifer Genealogy

for

The Thompson Sisters

Matilda Kay Thompson Walker

Judith Evelyn Thompson Witmer

Jo Ellen Thompson Lorenz

Elizabeth Nan Thompson Edmunds

The Daughters of Katherine Shields Pifer Thompson
and
Howard Vincent Thompson

The Grandaughters of John and Matilda Pifer
and
Howard J. and Elizabeth Thompson

Maternal Grandfather:	John Fredrick Pifer
Maternal Grandmother:	Matilda Adeline Smith Pifer
Paternal Grandfather:	Howard Jefferson Thompson
Paternal Grandmother:	Elizabeth Bailey Spencer Thompson

I would describe the Pifer family as **stalwart**—*strong, brave, and valiant.*
Mr. Leonard Kantar, a highly respected Curwensville businessman

ISBN 978-0-9837768-7-1

Published in the United States by Yesteryear Publishing.

Books are available at **www.amazon.com** as well as through the publisher:

Yesteryear Publishing

P.O. Box 311
Hummelstown, PA 17036

www.yesteryearpublishing.com

yesteryearpublishing@gmail.com
(717) 566-8655

Thompson-Pifer Genealogy: Thompson Sisters is an annotated genealogy tracing the lineage of four sisters through their two sets of grandparents from the time the ancestors landed in the 17th Century on the east coast of America from England, Germany, Scotland, Ireland or The Netherlands. There are four maternal and four paternal lineages included here, one of which connects the sisters to the 11th Century and William the Conqueror. Names and dates of births, marriages, and deaths are all listed with many generations' lineages enhanced by true personal stories and anecdotes that remind us of the struggles and very human characteristics not included in Family Trees and not always found in genealogies.

Researched and written by Judith Thompson Witmer

Page layout by E. Nan Thompson Edmunds

Table of Contents

Introduction

The Paternal Lineage for John F. Pifer is being used as the **baseline** for all of the genealogies in this book (**1.** Paternal: John; **2.** Maternal: John; **3.** Paternal: Matilda; **4.** Maternal: Matilda; **5.** Paternal: Howard; **6.** Maternal: Howard; **7.** Paternal: Elizabeth; **8.** Maternal: Elizabeth) because this paternal lineage for John Pifer holds the highest number (11) of generations who can be traced to their arrival in America. **The first generation either born or who arrived in America is being assigned the number "1."**

Each of the other seven lineages in this book also begins with a 1st generation for itself, followed by identification of how it aligns with this **baseline** (Paternal Lineage for John F. Pifer). For example, the first ancestor noted in each of the eight lineages is noted as **1st generation,** meaning it is first generation for a particular lineage. That first generation section is then compared to this **Paternal Lineage for John Pifer** and given a generation number that aligns the birth dates to where each generation would best fit on the lineage being used as the baseline. The red number following many of the names when they are first introduced shows the generation to which they belong.

Note: Information here—and in all of the eight genealogies in this booklet—is taken from many separate documents, written by different documenters, and from various sources. Information I could not find in family information, DAR applications, and *Straw's Genealogy,* I tried to find in newspapers articles and other material I have gathered over the years; I cross-checked all information with all other information. I then researched on Ancestry. com. While this website is helpful, one must remember than much of the information in the individual profiles that are available has been provided by families who are building their "family trees" and there are errors that even I as an amateur historian found. Further, the census reports and other government documents (birth, death, and marriage records) also contain errors because most of the information was gathered by citizen census takers and other list makers. In addition, it should be noted that information is fluid on these electronic sites. In addition, there is more than one spelling used for several of the ancestors. Choices of name spelling used were made by the author based on best evidence. Some place names were also known by different names.

It also should be noted that there is newly found information in these genealogies that is more accurate than that found in the books about our family, most recently, *The Story of Kate and Howard,* **2015.**

Paternal Lineage for John F. Pifer

"The Pifers"

1st generation in America

The Pifer ancestors came from Germany on the *Pink Mary* ship arriving September 29, 1733 in Philadelphia. Registered out of Dublin, the *Pink Mary* had taken on passengers at Rotterdam, then Plymouth, transferring 34 families of Palatinates (German and Swiss) to the new continent.

One hundred and seventy persons were qualified for clearances and very likely many became indentured servants for the next few years to pay for their passage to America.

It appears that the first identifiable Pifer ancestor to come to America was **Frequencki Dorflinger**[ii] (b. circa 1715 in The Netherlands; died March 11, 1769 in Northampton, Pennsylvania) who arrived in Philadelphia on the *Pink Mary* ship in 1733.

Frederick Dorflinger was the first generation of the Paternal Lineage of John Pifer, together with his wife Margaretta (no surname found) (b. 1719 in the Netherlands; d. August 22, 1758 in Upper Saucon Valley, Lehigh, Pennsylvania), and Frederick's sister Barbara (b. 1720; d. 1790)—all passengers on the *Pink Mary* ship.

Frederick Dorflinger married Margaretta (or, as I suspect, the name given [Margaretha] as the second wife is really the same Margaretta because the children's names and birthday are the same except for the addition of Catherina Elizabeth whose information is listed only with Margaretha.) A possible conclusion is that there was one wife and five daughters, although with such similar names among them, one must be skeptical.

    I.   **Maria Catherine** (b. 1738; d. 1803) (2nd)

    II.   Anna Maria (b. 1738; d. 1803). (Viewing the date of birth for both Anna Maria and Maria Catherine, there is a possibility that they were the same person or twins).

    III.   Anna Elizabeth (b. 1740; d. 1810)

    IV.   Mary Catherina (b. 1744; died 1804)

    V.   Catherina Elizabeth (b. December 24, 1750; d. 1803)

2nd generation in America

(Maria) Catherine (b. 1738; d. 1803 at Indian Creek, Lehigh, Pennsylvania) married **John** (Johannes) **Hancke** (b.1732; d. 1803). There is evidence that John Hancke (also spelled "Hankey") served in the Northampton County Militia in 1782, possibly having crossed the Delaware with General George Washington.

Maria Catherine Dorflinger and John Hancke were married on August 14, 1753 at St. Paul's Evangelical Lutheran. Church, Upper Saucon Township, Northampton, Pennsylvania and, while it is possible there were additional children born to them, are the parents of this child of record:

    Elizabeth (b. June 14, 1769 in Northampton County; d. November 25, 1842 in Greensburg, Pennsylvania) (3rd)

3rd generation

In 1785 at age sixteen **Elizabeth Hancke** married **Fredrick Pifer** (also spelled Fridrig Peiffer or Pfauffer) (b. 1766 in Northampton County; died November 24, 1808 in Westmoreland County).

This Fredrick Pifer is the first ancestor in this lineage with the Pifer name.

In 1790 Fredrick and Elizabeth Pifer, along with the families of John Hanke, Henry Best, and Fredrick Kuhns, were living as neighbors near the Lehigh River. Fredrick and Elizabeth then lived in Hempfield Township until they purchased land in Salem Township (Westmoreland County near Pittsburgh). By 1803 all members of this family were residing in Westmoreland County.

By the spring of 1805 Fredrick Pifer had purchased 210 acres in Westmoreland County where this family lived for three years at which time Fredrick died on November 24, 1808.

The child of record for Elizabeth Hancke and Fredrick Pifer is likely their second child

      (II.) John Fredrick (b. December 8, 1787; d. May 16, 1851) (4th)

There is also the possibility as recounted in one source that Elizabeth and Fredrick Pifer had additional children:

I.	Daniel	(b. 1786; d. 1819)
III.	George	(b. 1790; d. 1860)
IV.	Catherine	(b. 1794)
V.	Maria	(no available dates)
VI.	Barbara Elizabeth	(b. March 1, 1796; d. October 6, 1874)
VII.	Jonas	(b. 1797; d. 1860)
VIII.	Henry	(b. 1806)

If this is accurate, the story continues that Elizabeth Hancke (widow of Fredrick Pifer and mother of John F. Pifer) remarried in 1810, the same year that her son **John F.** married.

When (if) this Elizabeth re-married, two of the children (George and Daniel) of Elizabeth and Fredrick (her first husband) remained on the farm with their brother **John F.** The oldest daughter (Barbara) of Elizabeth and Fredrick had been married circa 1810-1811 (around the time of her widowed mother's second marriage) and lived with her husband.

The younger children of Elizabeth and Fredrick went with their mother Elizabeth when she remarried.

Elizabeth and her second husband, Jonathan Hile/Heyl (a widower), then had two children together, Sarah and Solomon.

4th generation

John Fredrick (John F. Pifer) (b. 1787 [or possibly 1789]; d. May 16, 1851) married **Charlotte Fry** (Frey, Frye) (b. July 25, 1791; d. November 18, 1875).

John was listed as living in Dauphin County and possibly was born there, but likely lived in Westmoreland by the date of his marriage. Records indicate that all of the children of John and Charlotte, except Thomas, were born in Westmoreland County.

John Fredrick Pifer and Charlotte Fry married in 1810 and are the parents of the following children:

I. Jonas (b. August 4, 1811; d. 1885) married Elizabeth Shetterly (b. 1817)

II. **John F.** (b. May 29, 1813 in Westmoreland County; d. April 28, 1899) (5th)
(Brothers Jonas and this John F. Pifer married sisters. This John F. is our lineage)

III. Simon Peter (b. 1815; d. 1822)
(This is the son *(see below)* who was just a child when he died as a result of an accident.)

IV. William Elias (b. December 27, 1817; d.1904)

V. George (b. 1820; d. 1900)

VI. Elizabeth (b. 1822; d. 1902)

VII. Mary A. (b. 1822; d. 1828) (possibly a twin to Elizabeth)

VIII. David (b. 1825)

IX. Maria Anna (b. 1829; d. 1844)

X. Thomas (b. 1832; d. 1907)

This John F. Pifer (son of Elizabeth and Fredrick), who had married Charlotte, farmed and also operated a still for additional income. In 1822, a lid on one of the vats blew, striking dead Simon Peter, John's seven-year-old son. John immediately gave up the brewery and invested in a herd of cattle, drove them to the Philadelphia market, only to discover that the market price of beef had fallen, resulting in a loss. The same experience happened with a herd of swine in which he next invested.

In 1829 John F. joined Fredrick Kuhnly (or Kuhns) in a move to the undeveloped wooded section of Jefferson County, now known as Henderson Township. The two families had bought 202 acres, at one dollar per acre, and divided it. John F. and his two sons John and Jonas took possession and erected a small log cabin, gradually making some improvements. This is said to have been in the Big-Run/ Paradise region of Jefferson County.

The remainder of John F.'s family joined him in December 1829, traveling by an oxen team pulling an old jumper sleigh bought especially because their son William had taken ill just before the departure. The weather was cold and the trip took seven days. Charlotte Fry Pifer, wife of John F., was remembered as a strong pioneer woman who is said to have killed a bear with her hoe when it disturbed her bee hives. Later, when she was near age 60, Charlotte is said to have bent a hickory rod with her bare hands, threatening her daughter-in-law, Betsy Zufall Pifer, who was told to never again use such a rod on her step-son (and Charlotte's grandson), young William T.

John F. Pifer took a leading part in local affairs, serving as County Commissioner and Justice of the Peace. He was said to be an intelligent man, as indicated by the carefully kept and well-written records of his judgments as township squire. His death, in 1851, was very sudden, occurring a half mile from Brookville while he was returning home with his son George.

George later succeeded his father as township squire and the records kept by both were later placed in the possession of George's grandson, Henry Pifer, an attorney in Harrisburg.

Both John F. and Charlotte are interred in the Rider graveyard one mile from their homestead, at the site of the old Paradise Lutheran Church. (John had assisted in building the log church which had preceded the Paradise Lutheran Church.)[1]

5th generation

This **John F. Pifer** (b. May 29, 1813; d. April 28, 1899) married Catherine Shetterly (b. 1817; d. November [or March] 30, 1889). Catherine was the daughter of Jacob Shetterly (b. 1779; d. 1846) and Maria Ann Gearhart (b. 1779; d. 1840).

John F. Pifer and Catherine Shetterly are the parents of the following children:

I.   **Jonas** (b. 1837/38; d. 1884, 1885, or 1894 [see note below]) (6th)

II.   William (b. 1840; d. 1917)

III.   John Calvin (b. August 1, 1841 [Ancestery.com]. Other sources give 1842 or 1843 as his date of birth.)

IV.   David Solomon (b. April 14, 1846; d. 1913)

V.   George W. (b. 1848/9)

VI.   Thomas (b. 1851)

VII.   Barbara Ann (b. December 11, 1852; d. October 17, 1942)

VIII. Alexander Jackson (Jack) (b. 1858)

6th generation

Jonas Pifer (b. 1837/38 in McCalmont Township; d. July 24, 1884 [Ancestry.com shows the date of death as March 20, 1885 and in another lineage as July 21, 1894] in Beaver Township, Jefferson County) married **Rachel Reed** (b. April 6/7, 1834/35; d. March 9, 1901), the daughter of Leah Peoples and Robert Reed. Jonas Pifer and Rachel Reed were married on September 29, 1859 and are the parents of the following children:

I.   Margaret Elenor (b. October 16, 1860/61)

II.   Joseph Reed (b. November 14, 1863; d. September 29, 1959 in Oregon)

III.   Hugh Millen (b. May 1865; d. 1920)

IV.   **John F.** (b. July 25, 1867/68)[iii]; d. May 3, 1954) (7th)

       (see progeny below)

VI.   Catherine/Kathryn (b. July 25, 1867/68) (John and Catherine were twins)
Catherine married William Shields of Brookville (b. 1869; d. 1935). Children:

    1. Dessie Isabelle (b. 1886; d. 1889)

    2. Henry Maxwell (b. 1896/97; date of death unknown)

       Wife: Agnes Harrison

       Daughter: Kathryn Ann

    3. John Lee (b. 1889; d. 1951)

    4. Catherine Princetta (b. 1902/03; date of death unknown)

       Husband: William A. Bowser (b. 1900)[iv]

       Son: William Shields (b. 1924; d. 1977 in Phoenix, Arizona)

VII. Jane (b. 1869; d. 1880)

VIII. Richard McClure (b. April 8, 1874; d. 1950 in Ontario)

7th generation

John F. Pifer (b. July 25, 1867/68 in Beaver Township, Jefferson County; d. May 3, 1954 in Curwensville) married **Matilda Adeline Smith** (b. June 2, 1872, also in Jefferson County; d. May 1, 1955 in Curwensville).

John F. Pifer and Matilda Adeline Smith, who wore the white wedding dress she had hand sewn,[v] were married on June 20, 1894. They are the parents of the following children:

I.   Josephine Smith (b. June 14, 1895 in Jefferson County; d. September 23, 1972) married Droz Hamilton (b. 1887; d. 1961) on December 20, 1919

       Noel Franklin (born 1934), living in Reston, Virginia (m. Karin G.)

       Two adopted children

II.   Ruby Idora (b. October 10, 1897 likely in Jefferson County; d. June 14, 1983 in Canton, Ohio); married in Punxsutawney in 1919 to Thomas Jefferson Wayne (b. June 30, 1898 in DuBois; d. August 13. 1975 in Ohio)

       John A. (b. April 18, 1924; d. March 25, 1994) (m. Nanette)

         Gregory

         Lisa

       Thomas J. (b. June 20, 1929; d. August 16, 1977)

         Thomas

         Mark

III.   Jessie Beverly (b. July 9, 1905 in Brockway; d. June 1, 1993 in Hershey); married Harry Hawes on March 21, 1930 and later married John Mohney on June 22, 1963

IV. **Katherine Shields** (b. February 11, 1908 in Curwensville; d. January 31, 1998 in Hummelstown/Hershey) (8th)
(see progeny below)

V. Margaret Jean (b. February 11, 1910 in Curwensville; d. December 30, 1958 in Clearfield); married A. Chester Bloom (b. December 12, 1908; d. November 13, 1993) in 1927.

> Chester Eugene (b. 1927) (m. Mable Riddle)
>> Mark
>> Debbie
> Donald Dwight (b. 1929) (m. Kathryn Lorraine Valimont)
> Janet Lynn (b. December 15, 1946), lives in Stafford, MO; (m. James C. Carter)
>> Shelly

8th generation

Kathryn Shields Pifer (b. February 11, 1908; died January 31, 1998) married **Howard V. Thompson** (b. April 10, 1904 in Clearfield; died January 14, 1964 in Clearfield).

Catherine S. Pifer (as her name appears on the marriage license)[vi] and Howard V. Thompson, Jr.[vii] were married on June 20, 1927 in Clearfield; the date was the 33rd wedding anniversary of her parents' marriage. Catherine and Howard are the parents of the following children:

I. **Matilda Kay** (b. November 1, 1930 in Curwensville) (9th)

II. **Judith Evelyn** (b. March 9, 1937 in Clearfield) (9th)

III. **Jo Ellen** (b. November 6, 1938 in Clearfield) (9th)

IV. **Elizabeth Nan** (b. August 19, 1942 in Clearfield) (9th)

9th generation

It was this generation who moved from Curwensville, each in turn after high school graduation: Kay moving to California, but returning to Curwensville in the late 1980s; Judith settling in Hummelstown, Pennsylvania to teach in the newly formed Lower Dauphin Junior-Senior High School; Jo Ellen leaving for government service and later working in her husband's CPA firm in the DC area; and Nan to DC, then California, returning to live in Hershey, Pennsylvania, where she worked in public relations and publications for the Penn State College of Medicine and Hershey Medical Center, now as designer for Yesteryear Publishing.

At this point the genealogies merge and become one with the Thompson Sisters who originate through the marriage of Catherine Pifer and Howard V. Thompson.

As explained in the section on the Paternal Lineage of John Frederick Pifer, which was used as the baseline, the genealogies are aligned by the ages of those who lived at a common time. Because a lineage begins with the first generation of a family that could be found, a person identified in the third generation of one lineage might match in age to those in the sixth generation of another's lineage. For example, in this set of genealogies, persons named in the seventh generation of Elizabeth's Paternal Lineage, would match in age with those in the eighth generation of John Pifer's Maternal Lineage as well as in his Paternal Lineage because his ancestors on both sides (mother and father) are of the same timeframe (similar birth dates).

Most frequently a person appears in different generations in the separate lineages. For example, because Matilda Pifer's mother's lineage could not be traced back very many generations (There are no records for the key people), Catherine and Howard Thompson are only the third generation in her Maternal Lineage, but are **eighth** in John Pifer's Maternal Lineage—or even **27**[th] if we count the lineage back to William the Conqueror.

To demonstrate, those of the **1**[st] **generation** of Matilda Smith Pifer's **Maternal Lineage** would align with the following:

- **4th generation** of her own **Paternal Lineage**
- **4th generation** of H. J. Thompson's **Paternal Lineage**
- **5th generation** of Elizabeth Spencer Thompson's **Paternal Lineage**
- **6th generation** of Elizabeth's **Maternal Lineage** and of H. J.'s **Maternal Lineage**
- **6th generation** of John F. Pifer's **Maternal Lineage** and **Paternal Lineage** beginning in America or the 25th generation (if we include to William the Conqueror) of his **Maternal Lineage**

THE THOMPSON SISTERS ARE

9th generation of Howard Jefferson Thompson's Maternal Lineage
7th generation of his Paternal Lineage

9th generation of Elizabeth Spencer Thompson's Maternal Lineage
8th generation of her Paternal Lineage

9th generation of John Frederick Pifer's Maternal Lineage
    (or 28th if we include back to William the Conqueror)
9th generation of his Paternal Lineage

4th generation of Matilda Smith Pifer's Maternal Lineage
7th generation of her Paternal Lineage

Matilda Kay

Following graduation Kay, a talented dancer, went to Philadelphia and auditioned for a place in a music hall/theatre chorus line. After a year in Philadelphia and being wooed by the man "back home," she returned to Curwensville. However, the call of far-away places led her to leave her hometown for California where she worked for Pacific Mutual and about a year later found her dream job with Trans World Airlines.

On August 26, 1950 **Matilda Kay Thompson** married **Albert R. Brunetti** (born June 12, 1924; d. August 19, 2012; son of Oreste and Edith Durandetto Brunetti). They are the parents of one child, a daughter, Mavis Kim, born on September 2, 1952. Following a divorce from Albert Brunetti, years later on May 22, 1980 Kay married **Robert A. Walker** of Clearfield.

The child of Kay Thompson and Albert Brunetti
> **Mavis Kim** (b. September 2, 1952 in Clearfield) (10th)

10th generation

Kim Richards lives in Cathedral City, California and is based in Palm Springs where she is a Buyer and Personal Shopper for Macy's. In 1970 Kim married Earl Richards, but the marriage later ended in divorce.

Judith Evelyn

Judith holds an earned doctorate in administration; served as a high school English teacher, principal, and assistant to the superintendent; worked for the Pennsylvania Department of Education; and is the Director of the Capital Area Institute for Mathematics and Science at Penn State Harrisburg. She also heads a private consulting business (Educon) and a publishing company (Yesteryear Publishing). In addition, she has chaired a number of major civic events and is the author of eighteen books, many on social history.

On September 6, 1958 **Judith Evelyn Thompson** (b. March 9, 1937) married **Thomas Eugene Ball** (b. January 31, 1937), son of Elmer and Rena Graham Ball. Following a divorce, on February 25, 1972 Judith married **Walter C. Witmer** (b. January 18, 1931; d. June 13, 2003), son of Miles and Ethel Espenshade Witmer).

The children of Judith Thompson and Thomas Ball
> I.   **Jean Rochelle Ball** (b. March 7, 1959 in Harrisburg) (10th)
> II. **Thomas Ross Ball** (b. April 23, 1968 in Camp Hill) (10th)

10th generation

Jean Rochelle Ball Jacobs is the staff accountant for Kurtz Bros. in Clearfield, Pennsylvania. She married James Gary Jacobs (b. October 3, 1948) in 1984.

The children of Jean Rochelle Ball and James Jacobs

     I.   **Jordan Ashlee** (b. April 17, 1986 in Clearfield) (11th)

     II.   **Jillian Rochelle** (b. October 29, 1992 in Clearfield) (11th)

Thomas Ross Ball is the owner of Thomas Ball Entertainment in Hershey, Pennsylvania. He married **Michelle Ann Garger** (b. 1971) in 2000; they were divorced in 2015. The children of Thomas Ross Ball and Michelle Garger

     I.   **Emily Madison** (b. July 11, 2002 in Harrisburg) (11th)

     II.   **Olivia Emerson** (b. June 27, 2005 in Harrisburg) (11th)

11th generation

As of September 2015:

    Jordan Ashlee Jacobs is employed by Laborers Int'l. Union of North America 158 HCL.

    Jillian Rochelle Jacobs is Hospital Operations Coordinator for United Health Services.

    Emily Madison Ball is in eighth grade at the Lower Dauphin Middle School.

    Olivia Emerson Ball is in fifth grade at Conewago Elementary School.

Jo Ellen

Jo Ellen began her professional career with the Federal Bureau of Investigation (FBI) in Washington, DC, followed by a position with the National Security Agency (the top intelligence organization of the U.S. government), then the newest government agency—later to become the premium agency with the highest clearances required—where she quickly earned a high-level administrative position. She later joined her husband in his business, Lorenz and Lorenz Certified Public Accountants.

On September 6, 1958, in a double wedding ceremony shared with her sister Judith, **Jo Ellen Thompson** (b. November 6, 1938) married **Eugene Kendall Lorenz** (b. September 19, 1932), the son of Alma ("Bonnie") Corinne Miller and Eugene Hurdle Lorenz.

The children of Jo Ellen Thompson and Eugene Kendall Lorenz

     I.   **Janelle Corinne Lorenz Wright** (b. January 2, 1969) (10th)

     II. **Eugene Kendall Lorenz, Jr.** (b. April 17, 1970; d. January 3, 2013) (10th)

10th generation

Janelle Lorenz Wright manages real estate for her parents and her family. Previously, she was employed by KPMG Peat Marwick and as the private label buyer for Saks Fifth Avenue's catalog division.

Janelle Lorenz married **Jay Oscar Wright** (b. December 12, 1969, St. Johnsbury, Vermont) on October 25, 1997. They reside in Potomac, Maryland. They are the parents of

     I. **Corinne Catherine Wright** (b. May 29, 2001 in Sarasota, Florida) (11th)

     II. **Theodore Piers Wright** (b. September 30, 2002 in Silver Spring, Maryland) (11th)

11th generation

As of September 2015:

> **Corinne Catherine Wright** is in the ninth grade at The Connelly School of the Holy Child, Potomac, Maryland.

> **Theodore Piers Wright** is in the sixth grade at Echelon Academy, Sandy Spring, Maryland.

Elizabeth Nan

Nan began her professional career with the National Security Agency in Washington, DC. She later moved to Southern California where she worked for the City of Anaheim. Following a return to Pennsylvania, she worked in Development for Dickinson College in Carlisle before finding her niche in Public Relations for Penn State's College of Medicine and Hershey Medical Center. Currently she manages and is the page designer for Yesteryear Publishing.

On August 18, 1965 **Elizabeth Nan Thompson** (b. August 19, 1942) married **Joel Keith Edmunds** (b. August 14, 1942), the son of Irvin C. and Jaclyn Beck Edmunds.

The children of Elizabeth Nan Thompson and Joel Keith Edmunds

> I.   **Shayne Scott Edmunds** (b. December 9, 1965 in Northridge, California) (10th)

> II. **Jesse Joel Edmunds** (b. November 6, 1979 in Lucerne Valley, California) (10th)

10th generation

Shayne Edmunds and his wife, **Grace Graybill,** are co-owners of the Neato Burrito restaurant chain located throughout South Central Pennsylvania.

Shayne Edmunds married **Ada Grace Graybill** (b. November 10, 1969) on June 15, 1999. They reside in Dillsburg, Pennsylvania and are the parents of

> I.   **Aero Graham** (b. April 18, 2004 in Harrisburg, Pennsylvania) (11th)

> II. **Iris Isadora** (b. September 2, 2005 in Harrisburg, Pennsylvania) (11th)

Jesse Edmunds is an outdoor adventurer as well as an accomplished musician who currently performs in the Greater Harrisburg, Pennsylvania area. He resides in Hershey, Pennsylvania.

11th generation

As of September 2015:

> **Aero Graham** is in the sixth grade at Northern Middle School in Dillsburg, Pennsylvania.

> **Iris Isadora** is in the fifth grade at Northern Elementary School in Dillsburg, Pennsylvania.

i   Also spelled Fredrich and Friederich

ii   Also spelled Durflinger

iii   There are inconsistencies throughout with the birth date of John F. Pifer; the memory card at his memorial service gave the birth date as 1886, which is obviously a misprint and was intended to be 1868; Ancestry.com uses 1867.

iv   It was this gentleman's daughter or perhaps daughter-in-law who sent a note to my mother (who would have been a cousin to Catherine Princetta) of Catherine Princetta's passing. At the time my mother wondered who this Mrs. Bowser was. As I recall, there was no return address, just a postmark on the envelope.

v   This dress is framed and still in the possession of the family.

vi   Mother told us that this is the spelling Howard used and she continued with it.

vii   Howard used the "Jr." designation even though his middle name was not that of his father.

Maternal Lineage

for

John F. Pifer

Maternal Lineage for John F. Pifer

"The Reeds"

The following is an expanded account of the maternal lineage of John F. Pifer, the maternal grandfather of Kay, Judith, Jo Ellen, and Nan Thompson. John F. Pifer's Maternal Lineage is the longest of the eight lineages we have traced, providing a count of **30 generations,** beginning in the early 11th Century. The first 19 generations in this document are listed (and, in some cases, explained) but are not part of the **11 generations traced in this and the other seven lineages, all of which are numbered based on living in America.**

There is evidence that our ancestry through Rachel Reed, John Pifer's mother, is directly descended from **William the Conqueror.** This lineage from the 11th Century to the 18th Century will be presented in Part I. Part II will begin with the more detailed story beginning with **Margaret Oliphant and her husband Thomas Gordon, the first generation of John Pifer's ancestors to be born in America.** The names of verified ancestors are bolded. Names that are boxed are questionable as to dates or lack of verification, but are included, as these names may offer leads in the complete or future genealogical record.

As might be expected, the dates found do not always align neatly. I have tried to take into account the general dates of the child-bearing women, making adjustments where noted in order to make the dates more credible. I left the dates found on the source Jay Wright used, but also added new dates (my adjustments) as I discovered them.

It also should be stated that there is newly found information and clarification in these genealogies that is more accurate than that found in the books about our family, including *Jebbie: Vamp to Victim: The Truth About Miss Pifer* (2011); *Growing Up Silent in the 1950s; Not All Tailfins and Rock 'n' Roll* (2012); *All the Gentlemen Callers: Letters from a 1920s Steamer Trunk* (2012), and, most recently, *The Story of Kate and Howard,* (2015).

Part I

(1) William the Conqueror (b. October 14, 1027; d. September 9, 1087) is the son of Robert I, Duke of Normandy and Harlette de Falaise. William was born in Falaise, Normandy, France. Other names (titles) he holds are William of Normandy and William I, King of England.

William the Conqueror of Normandy married Matilda of Flanders in 1053 in Cathedral de Notre Dame, Normandy (*Normandie*), France. Matilda was the daughter of Baldwin V, de Lille, Count of Flanders and Adele Capet, Princess of France (b. 1000; d. 1078/09), who was the daughter of Robert II of France.

Matilda was born circa 1032 in Flanders and died November 2, 1083 in Caen, Normandy, France. She is sometimes referred to as Maud of Flanders. **She also was a seventh generation direct descendent of Alfred the Great** (which could raise our traceable generations to 37). Matilda's marriage to William strengthened his claim to the throne. All sovereigns of England, Great Britain, and the United Kingdom have been descended from her, as has the present (as of 2015) Queen Elizabeth II.

The children of William and Matilda (not all verified)

I.	Robert Curthose	VI.	Adella
II.	Adeliza (Alice)	VII.	Agatha
III.	Cecilia	VIII.	Constance
IV.	William Rufus	IX.	Matilda (?)
V.	Richard, Duke of Bernay	X.	**Henry Beauclerc**

▼

(2) Henry (Beauclerc) I, King of England (b. May 1068/69; d. December 1, 1135) was born in Winchester, Hampshire (also listed as Selby, Yorkshire) and died in St. Denis-le-Fermont, France. Henry I is said to have sired 24 children to two different wives and several mistresses. He was the fourth son of William the Conqueror, succeeding his elder brother William III as King of England in 1100 and defeating his eldest brother Robert Curthose to become Duke of Normandy in 1106.

Henry I had a number of marriages and many relationships. A relationship with Elizabeth de Beaumont (or possibly with Nesta, Princess of Wales), without marriage, resulted in at least one child, Elizabeth, the offspring of record.

▼

(3) Elizabeth, Princess of England was born in 1095 in Yorkshire, England. She married Fergus, Lord of Galloway (b. circa 1090; d. 1161 in Edinburgh, Scotland) in 1124 in Carrick, Ayrshire, Scotland.

The children of Princess Elizabeth and Lord Fergus

    I. Uchtred, Lord of Galloway (b. circa 1120 in Carrick Ayrshire, Scotland; d. September 22, 1174)

        ■ Uchtred's son: Roland (Lochlann), Lord of Galloway (b. 1135[52]; d. December 19, 1200) in Northamptonshire, England, married Elena De Morville in 1172.

    II.   Gilbert of Galloway (Carrick) (b. circa 1126; d. January 1185)

    III.   Affrica of Galloway (b. 1128)

    IV.   **Margaret De Galloway** (b. 1130 [**1140** is more likely considering her child for this lineage is noted as being born in 1179, which I selectively am changing to **1174**); d. 1182), born in Ayrshire, Scotland

▼

(4) Margaret De Galloway married Alan FitzWalter (b. circa 1126; d. 1204) of Renfrewshire, Scotland.

The children of Margaret Galloway and Alan FitzWalter

    I.   Walter Steward (b. circa 1161; d. 1241)

    II.   **Avelina (b. 1174; d. 1202)**

    III.   David (b. circa 1182) (This date would be highly unlikely if Margaret had been born in 1130.)

▼

(5) Avelina FitzWalter (b. 1174/79; d. 1202), born in Paisley, Renfrewshire, Scotland, married Duncan, 1st Earl of Carrick (b. circa 1174 in Galloway, Scotland; d. June 13, 1252).

The children of Avelina FitzWalter and Duncan Carrick

    I.   A daughter

    II.   **Neil, Earl of Carrick** (b. 1202; d. 1256)

▼

(6) Neil, Earl of Carrick was born in Carrick, Ayrshire, Scotland. In 1255 (or 1250) he married Margaret Stewart (b. 1230).

The child of Neil Carrick and Margaret Stewart

    I.   **Margaret, Countess of Carrick** (b. 1252; d. October 27, 1292)

▼

(7) Margaret of Carrick married Robert Bruce, the 6th Robert Bruce, Earl of Carrick (b. July 1243 in Dumfrieshire, Scotland; d. March 4, 1304). They were married in 1271 in Turnberry Castle, Essex, England.

Among the ten children of Margaret Carrick and Robert Bruce was

    II.   **Robert the Bruce** (the 7th by this name) (b. July 11, 1274; d. June 7, 1329).

▼

(8) The 7th Robert the Bruce married Elizabeth de Burgh in his second marriage. Elizabeth de Burgh (b. 1284; d. October 27, 1327) was born in Ireland, the daughter of the powerful Richard Óg de Burgh, 2nd Earl of Ulster and his wife Margarite de Burgh (died 1304).

On March 27, 1306, Robert and Elizabeth de Burgh were crowned King and Queen of Scots at Scone. Their youngest daughter was **Elizabeth Bruce.** (No date was found, but I am assigning it circa 1317 based on when she later married and gave birth.)

(9) Elizabeth Bruce married **Sir Walter Oliphant, Lord Aberdalgie** (b. circa 1324; d. 1378), son of Sir William Oliphant.

The child of Elizabeth Bruce (assigning her birth date as 1317 makes her 23 at the birth of this child) and Sir Walter Oliphant.

> **Sir John Oliphant** (b. 1340; d. 1417/20) of Aberdalgie

▼

(10) Sir John Oliphant married Filia Borthwick (b. 1346; d. 1410) from Borthwick, Midlothian, Scotland.

The child of Sir John Oliphant and Filia Borthwick (this would have her age as 25 at this time)

> **Sir William Oliphant** (b. 1371; d. 1425)

▼

(11) Sir William Oliphant married Marian de Berwick, daughter of Thomas de Berwick. In 1417 he was sent to London as a hostage for the ransom of King James I; his name disappeared from records after 1425.

The child of Sir William Oliphant and Marian de Berwick

> **Sir John Oliphant** (b. circa 1410; d. January 23, 1445/46)

▼

(12) Sir John Oliphant of Aberdalgie married Margaret Ogilvy (b. circa 1415; died after 1471), daughter of Sir Patrick Ogilvy of Auchterhouse. Sir John was killed in battle.

Among the six children of Sir John Oliphant and Margaret Ogilvy (at age 24)

> **Laurence Oliphant, 1st Lord Oliphant** (b. circa 1439; d. 1499)

▼

(13) Baron Laurence Oliphant married Lady Isabel Hay (b. [dates found were 1430 and 1441; it is likely that the date would be at least 1435]; d. 1471) daughter of William Hay, 1st Earl of Erroll and Lady Beatrix Douglas.

Among the six children of Laurence Oliphant and Isabel Hay

> **John Oliphant, 2nd Lord Oliphant** (b. 1460; d. 1515)

▼

(14) John Oliphant married Lady Elizabeth Isabel Campbell (b. 1458; d. 1493), daughter of Colin Campbell, 1st Earl of Argyll and Isabel Stewart. John succeeded to the title of **2nd Lord Oliphant** before 1500 at which time he then served as heir to his father.

There is lack of detailed evidence of the following two ancestors; however, their names are left here for future matching.

▼

Place-holder numbers are being used here, as there **are** ancestors (even if not these two gentlemen)—more likely three generations between John [14 above] and Laurence [17 below]. Considering child-bearing ages of the women, it is likely that **three** generations should be covered in this block of unknowns.

(15) William Oliphant (b. 1493); married Margaret in 1513

▼

(16) Laurence Oliphant (b. 1530); married Mary Rollo (b. circa 1542)

▼

(17) Laurence Oliphant (b. 1610;[i] d. July 20, 1679) married Lilias Graeme (b. 1608) in 1634. Both Laurence and Lilias are part of the Oliphants of Gask in Scotland.

The children of Laurence and Lilias

I.   Laurence (b. 1634 in Gask; d. July 20, 1679), 3rd Earl of Gask

II.   John Oliphant (b. 1635) married Janet Gilchrist (b. 1648; d. 1685 [or 1700, the date in Ancestry.com])

        (See chart information below in box.)

III.   **David Oliphant** (b. 1649 in Perth, Scotland; d. November 2, 1707. Using this date of birth, David's mother would have been 41, so the date here may be in error.)

▼

(18) David Oliphant (b. 1649 in Perthshire, Scotland; d. November 2, 1707 in Edinburgh)

For years it was thought that John Oliphant (2nd son of Laurence and Lilias) was the father of Duncan Oliphant (below), but recent findings (Bobby J. Chamberlain, October 1, 2005, in Genealogy.com) now support that **Duncan was the son of David Oliphant**, the brother of John. Because this information on David is recent, his name does not appear either in the list from which I am working (provided by Jay Wright) or with any substantiation in additional online searches at this time. However, we will accept this finding of Ms. Chamberlain for our purposes.

David Oliphant's children are listed in Carney Family Genealogy pages online[ii]

Further, the following information needs to be considered by the reader regarding dates and events for **Janet Gilchrist** (wife of John Oliphant, or possibly David Oliphant):

- Born 1648 in Scotland

- Gave birth at age 15 to her first child, William, 1663

- Gave birth at age 16 to her second child, Margaret, 1664

- Gave birth at age 19 to her third child, Janet, 1667
- Married in 1670 to **either** the Reverend John Oliphant (b. 1635 or 1640) **or** David Oliphant (b. 1649). Consider this in light of the supposition given in (18) above (and the fact that we have no name for a wife of David).
- Gave birth in 1682 to son Duncan (b. 1682; d. 1734)

Further research and substantiation will be needed for confirmation. At present the genealogy charts for this family on Ancestry.com is limited to their own family members, so I could not fully confirm the information.

▼

(19) Duncan Oliphant (b. 1682; d. August 7, 1734) was born in Perthshire, Scotland; he reportedly arrived in Staten Island around 1695. In 1705 (also in Staten Island) Duncan married **Mary Garrison** (b. 1686 in Scotland; also died August 7, 1734 in Hunterdon County, New Jersey, according to the Carney Family Genealogy). Mary is the daughter of Lambert Garrison (1655-1725) and Susanna Morgan (1655-1715).

Duncan Oliphant and Mary Garrison were the parents of one daughter **Margaret Oliphant** (b. April 19, 1709; d. June [or September] 3, 1784 in Staten Island, New York).

Another source indicated that Duncan Oliphant and Mary Garrison had 12 children, 10 of whom were named.

I. David (b. 1706; d. 1707)
II. Margaret (b. 1709; d. September 5, 1784)
III. David (b. March 1, 1712; d. September 3, 1774)
IV. John (b. 1715; d. sometime after 1756)
V. Ephraim (b. 1717; d. 1795)
VI. James (b. 1719; d. June 17, 1816)
VII. Mary (b. 1721; d. unknown)
VIII. Ann (b. 1723; d. unknown)
IX. Jonathan (b. 1726; d. unknown)
X. Samuel (b. 1728; d. unknown)

This source also suggested that Margaret Oliphant married James Clifford and that they were the parents of Charles Clifford. This information is included here to show that various family trees have conflicting information and to suggest a possible family connection.

Part II

1st generation (20th if we include the above European lineage to William the Conqueror)

Margaret Oliphant, born on Staten Island, married **Thomas Gordon** (b. 1696 in Staten Island; d. June 1784 in Amwell, Hunterdon, New Jersey), thus becoming the **1st generation of John Pifer's Maternal Lineage in America.**

The parents of Thomas Gordon were Thomas Gordon (b. 1652 in Aberdeenshire, Scotland; d. 1722 in Monmouth, New Jersey) and Janet Mudie (b. 1654 in Aberdeenshire, Scotland; d. 1744 in Monmouth, New Jersey).

Margaret Oliphant and Thomas Gordon were married in 1731 in Hunterdon County, New Jersey and are the parents of two daughters

     I.   Epenetus (b. 1732; d. September 9, 1821), named for her father's sister

    II. **Jane** (b. 1738 in Hunterdon, New Jersey; d. 1802 in Ligonier Valley, Westmoreland County) (2nd)

2nd generation (or 21st)

Jane Gordon married **Charles Clifford, Sr.** (b. November 10, 1730 in Bethlehem Township, Hunterdon County, New Jersey; d. January 1, 1816 in Westmoreland County, Pennsylvania). They were married on March 4, 1757.

> Dates of birth cohorts place Charles Clifford "parallel" in age to those of the second generation from the lineage of Frederick Durflinger who was the first generation ancestor of John F. Pifer's paternal lineage. This is how the generations were determined for these 8 genealogies of the Thompson sisters.
>
> - Dorflinger (paternal lineage) was born in 1711 and Margaret Oliphant (maternal lineage)was born in 1709 making them of the same age generation.
> - Maria Catherine (Dorflinger's daughter), the second generation, was born in 1738 and Charles Clifford was born in 1730 making them of the same age generation.

In the spring of 1759 Charles Clifford (age about 29) moved from New Jersey and took up a homestead tract in Westmoreland County, Pennsylvania which remained in the family at least until the time of the Daughters of the American Revolution membership application (c. 1960s) for which this early genealogical information originally was provided to Jessie B. Pifer.

Charles Clifford, described as a Revolutionary patriot, assisted in the building of Fort Ligonier[iii] and was captured by Indians near the fort on April 22, 1779. Boucher's *History of Westmoreland County* notes that a party of Indians fired at him, the bullets passing through his hat and clothes and one ball splintering his gun barrel and cutting his face. Charles Clifford served on the frontier and his name appears on the muster rolls of the third battalion, according to the Westmoreland County Archives.[iv]

The records further show that Clifford served as a Private in the Westmoreland County militia. His name appears on a return list, dated "Quebec, November 8, 1782," of the prisoners sent to the province of Quebec for exchange beginning the first of November 1779. This also shows that Charles (who would have been 51 years old at the time of the event) was sent September 1781 by way of Lake Champlain.

3ʳᵈ generation (or 22ⁿᵈ) (if compared to the ages of the 3ʳᵈ generation [Elizabeth, 1767] in John Pifer's Paternal Lineage)

The 3ʳᵈ generation would be the children of Charles Clifford and Jane Gordon who were married, according to records, on March 1737.

I. Edward (b. 1755; d. 1833) (unknown spouse) (Noting the date of the marriage of Charles and Jane in March 1757 the birth date here of Edward may be in error.)

II. James (b. 1758; d. 1801 (married Mary Rogers?)

III. Thomas (b. 1760; died 1875) (married Catherine Lawson?)

IV. Robert (b. 1760; died 1791) (unknown spouse) (Thomas and Robert likely were twins.)

V. Mary (b. 1762; died 1801) (married James Whiteside?)

VI. Joseph (b. 1764; d. 1841) (married Isabel Pritchet?)

VII. Thomas (b. 1764; d. 1842) (this would be unlikely having a second child by the same name, yet he is listed as a twin to Joseph)

VIII. Edward (b. 1768; no date of death given) (again, unlikely having an older sibling by the same name)

IX. Charles (b. 1770; d. 1833) (Another source gives the following information for Charles: b. 1764 and married Jennie Lytle)

X. Mary (b. 1771 [again a question as to reusing the name])

XI. Jane (b. September 1772 [possibly 1762]; d. November 12, 1852) (married John Menoher?)

XII. Sarah Sally (b. July 4, 1776; d. November 17, 1853) (married Robert Pomeroy Reed) (designated 4ᵗʰ generation)

The presumed (based on ages) 4ᵗʰ generation (or 23ʳᵈ)

Given the wide range of age (21 years) between the Clifford siblings Edward (1755) and Sarah (1776), if we consider Sarah as the 4ᵗʰ generation the "ages" and "years of birth" of the personages can be aligned more closely throughout the generations. Further, when compared to the ages of those of the 4ᵗʰ generation in the John Pifer Paternal Lineage (and, in fact, all of the eight lineages in this book), Sarah Clifford (b. 1776) will herein be viewed as 4ᵗʰ generation by age of birth.

Sarah Sally Clifford (b. July 4, 1776; d. November 7, 1853) married **Robert Pomeroy Reed, Sr.** (b. 1772; d. October 17, 1849). Robert was born in Ligonier. In 1778, Robert's brother George (b. 1756) was killed by Indians, while George's twin sister Mattie (b. 1756; d. 1789) was able to outrun them.

> There is a Robert Reed (b. 1730; d. 1796) of Scottish ancestry who married Mary "Polly" Pomeroy (b. 1731; d. 1803) of Donegal, Ireland. They are the parents of Robert Pomeroy Reed, Sr. (above) who married Sarah Sally Clifford.

Sarah Sally Clifford and Robert Pomeroy Reed were married on June 1, 1793 in Cumberland Valley, Pennsylvania; they are the parents of the following children. (Some accounts suggest that Sarah and Robert were the parents of 15 children. The questionable one has been placed here in italics.)

    I.   Joseph Reed (b. 1793; d. 1799)

    II.   Polly Mary Reed (b. August 14, 1794; d. 1872/79)

    III.   Charles Reed (b. September 29, 1796; d. 1860)

    IV.   George Reed (b. 1798; d. 1799)

    V.   *James Reed (b. 1801; d. 1802)*

    VI.   James Reed (b. March 15, 1801; d. 1870) (One can only speculate that there may have been twins born, with one dying a year after birth, and perhaps a name was changed. Records were not always accurate.

    VII.   **Robert Reed** (b. October 30, 1804; d. January 20, 1865) (5th)

    VIII.   Sarah (Sally) Reed (b. November 7, 1806/07: d. 1873)

    IX.   Margaret Reed (b. November 4, 1807; d. 1881)

    X.   John Reed (b. May 28, 1808; d. 1881)

    XI.   Joseph Reed (b. 1809)

    XII.   Samuel Reed (b. 1810; d. 1869)

    XIII.   Thomas Clifford Reed (b. August 16, 1813; d. 1878)

    XIV.   Lavinia (b. January 26, 1816; d. 1889)

    XV.   Marshall (b. May 15, 1819; d. 1892)

5th generation (or 24th) (aligns with that of the John Pifer Paternal Lineage)

Robert Reed, Jr. (b. October 30, 1804; d. January 20, 1865) (grandfather to "our" grandfather John F. Pifer) married **Leah Peoples** (b. 1803; d. December 15, 1845 in Brookville). Leah's parents were Leah and Thomas Peoples.

Robert Reed and Leah Peoples were married July 11, 1833 at Ligonier Valley, Westmoreland County; they are the parents of the following:

    I.   **Rachel Reed** (b. April 6, 1835; d. March 9, 1901) (6th)

II.   Joseph Lorenza (b. March 9, 1840; d. February 2, 1884)

III.   Sarah Ellen ("Sadie") (b. September 21, 1842; d. August 16, 1922). She married John Calvin Pifer, the son of Catherine Shetterly and John F. Pifer (b. 1813). Sadie and John Calvin are the parents of Vincent King Pifer (b. January 29, 1876 in Jefferson County; d. 1965 in Hallwood, Accomack, Virginia); thus, John Pifer (b. 1867/8) and King Pifer, a newspaper editor, are cousins as I had surmised in earlier writings.[v]

It is at this 6ᵗʰ generation point that the Paternal and Maternal Lineages of John F. Pifer merge.

6ᵗʰ generation (or 25ᵗʰ) (aligns with that of the John Pifer Paternal Lineage)

Rachel Reed (b. April 6, 1835; d. March 9, 1901 in Brookville), married **Jonas Pifer** (b. June 4, 1837/38 in McCalmont Township; d. July 24, 1884. [Ancestry.com shows the date of death as March 20, 1885 and another lineage source provides the date July 21, 1894 in Beaver Township, Jefferson County.])

Rachel Reed and Jonas Pifer were married on September 29, 1859, lived in McCalmont Township, Jefferson County, and are the parents of the following children:

I.   Margaret Elenor (b. October 16, 1860/61)

II.   Joseph Reed (b. November 14, 1863; d. September 29, 1959 in Oregon)

III.   Hugh Millen (or Hugh W.) (b. May 1865; d. 1920)

IV.   **John Frederick** (b. July 25, 1867/68[vi]; d. May 3, 1954) **(7ᵗʰ)**
        (see progeny below)

V.   Catherine/Kathryn (b. July 25, 1867/68) (John and Catherine were twins)
        Catherine married William Shields (b. 1859 in Brookville; d. 1935)
        Their children
        1. Dessie Isabelle (b. 1886; d. 1889)

        2. Henry Maxwell (b. 1896/97; date of death unknown)
           Wife: Agnes Harrison
           Daughter: Kathryn Ann

        3. John Lee (b. 1889; d. 1951)

        4. Catherine Princetta (b. 1902/03; date of death unknown)
           Husband: William A. Bowser (b. 1900)[vii]
           Son: William Shields Bowser (b. 1924; d. 1977 in Phoenix, Arizona)

VI.   Jane (b. 1869/71; d. 1880)

VII.   Richard McClure (b. April 8, 1873/74; d. 1950 in Ontario)

(Rachel Reed Pifer did not live to see all of her grandchildren, including Jessie, Katherine, and Margaret Jean, daughters of her son John F. Pifer. Further, since Matilda's mother also had died young—and before her daughters bore children, these three younger daughters of John and Matilda had no experience of grandmothers. It makes me wonder where our mother learned such love and personal interest and interaction with her own grandchildren.)

John F. Pifer is the offspring of the joining of his Maternal and Paternal Lineages in the 6th generation.

7th generation (or 26th) (aligns with that of the John Pifer Paternal Lineage)

John F. Pifer (b. July 25, 1867/68 in Beaver Township, Jefferson County; d. May 3, 1954 in Curwensville) married **Matilda Adeline Smith** (b. June 2, 1872, also in Jefferson County; d. May 1, 1955 in Curwensville).

John F. Pifer and Matilda Adeline Smith, who wore the white wedding dress she had hand sewn[viii], were married on June 20, 1894. They are the parents of the following children:

I. Josephine Smith (b. June 14, 1895 in Jefferson County; d. September 23, 1972) married Droz Hamilton (b. 1887; d. 1961) on December 20, 1919
    Noel Franklin (born 1934), living in Reston, Virginia (m. Karin G.)
        Two adopted children

II. Ruby Idora (b. October 10, 1897 likely in Jefferson County; d. June 14, 1983 in Canton, Ohio); married in Punxsutawney in 1919 to Thomas Jefferson Wayne (b. June 30, 1898 in DuBois; d. August 13. 1975 in Ohio)
    John A. (b. April 18, 1924; d. March 25, 1994) (m. Nanette)
        Gregory and Lisa
    Thomas J. (b. June 20, 1929; d. August 16, 1977)
        Thomas and Mark

III. Jessie Beverly (b. July 9, 1905 in Brockway; d. June 1, 1993 in Hershey); married Harry Hawes on March 21, 1930 and later married John Mohney on June 22, 1963

IV. **Katherine Shields** (b. February 11, 1908 in Curwensville; d. January 31, 1998 in Hummelstown/Hershey) (8th)
    (see progeny below)

V. Margaret Jean (b. February 11, 1910 in Curwensville; d. December 30, 1958 in Clearfield); married A. Chester Bloom (b. December 12, 1908; d. November 13, 1993) in 1927.
    Chester Eugene (b. 1927) (m. Mable Riddle)
        Mark and Debbie
    Donald Dwight (b. 1929) (m. Kathryn Lorraine Valimont)
    Janet Lynn (b. December 15, 1946), lives in Stafford, MO; (m. James C. Carter)
        Shelly

8th generation (or 27th) (aligns with that of the John Pifer Paternal Lineage)

Kathryn Shields Pifer (b. February 11, 1908; died January 31, 1998) married **Howard V. Thompson** (b. April 10, 1904 in Clearfield; died January 14, 1964 in Clearfield).

Catherine S. Pifer (as her name appears on the marriage license)[9] and Howard V. Thompson, Jr.[10] were married on June 20, 1927 in Clearfield; the date was the 33rd wedding anniversary of her parents' marriage. Catherine and Howard are the parents of the following children:

I.   **Matilda Kay** (b. November 1, 1930 in Curwensville) **(9th)**

II.   **Judith Evelyn** (b. March 9, 1937 in Clearfield) **(9th)**

III.   **Jo Ellen** (b. November 6, 1938 in Clearfield) **(9th)**

IV.   **Elizabeth Nan** (b. August 19, 1942 in Clearfield) **(9th)**

9th generation (or 28th) (aligns with that of the John Pifer Paternal Lineage)

It was this generation who moved from Curwensville, each in turn after high school graduation: Kay moving to California, but returning to Curwensville in the late 1980s; Judith settling in Hummelstown, Pennsylvania to teach in the newly formed Lower Dauphin Junior-Senior High School; Jo Ellen leaving for government service and later working in her husband's CPA firm in the DC area; and Nan to DC, then California, returning to live in Hershey, Pennsylvania, where she worked in public relations and publications for the Penn State Medical Center, now as designer for Yesteryear Publishing.

At this point the genealogies merge and become one with the Thompson Sisters who originate through the marriage of Catherine Pifer and Howard V. Thompson.

As explained in the section on the Paternal Lineage of John Frederick Pifer, which was used as the baseline, the genealogies are aligned by the ages of those who lived at a common time. Because a lineage begins with the first generation of a family that could be found, a person identified in the third generation of one lineage might match in age to those in the sixth generation of another's lineage. For example, in this set of genealogies, persons named in the seventh generation of Elizabeth's Paternal Lineage, would match in age with those in the eighth generation of John Pifer's Maternal Lineage as well as in his Paternal Lineage because his ancestors on both sides (mother and father) are of the same timeframe (similar birth dates).

Most frequently a person appears in different generations in the separate lineages. For example, because Matilda Pifer's mother's lineage could not be traced back very many generations (There are no records for the key people), Catherine and Howard Thompson are only the third generation in her Maternal Lineage, but are **eighth** in John Pifer's Maternal Lineage—or even **27th** if we count the lineage back to William the Conqueror.

To demonstrate, those of the **1ˢᵗ generation** of Matilda Smith Pifer's **Maternal Lineage** would align with the following:

- **4th generation** of her own **Paternal Lineage**

- **4th generation** of H. J. Thompson's **Paternal Lineage**

- **5th generation** of Elizabeth Spencer Thompson's **Paternal Lineage**

- **6th generation** of Elizabeth's **Maternal Lineage** and of H. J.'s **Maternal Lineage**

- **6th generation** of John F. Pifer's **Maternal Lineage** and **Paternal Lineage** beginning in America or the 25th generation (if we include to William the Conqueror) of his **Maternal Lineage**

THE THOMPSON SISTERS ARE

9th generation of Howard Jefferson Thompson's Maternal Lineage
7th generation of his Paternal Lineage

9th generation of Elizabeth Spencer Thompson's Maternal Lineage
8th generation of her Paternal Lineage

9th (or 28th if we include back to William the Conqueror) generation of John Frederick Pifer's Maternal Lineage
9th generation of his Paternal Lineage

4th generation of Matilda Smith Pifer's Maternal Lineage
7th generation of her Paternal Lineage

Matilda Kay

Following graduation Kay, a talented dancer, went to Philadelphia and auditioned for a place in a music hall/theatre chorus line. After a year in Philadelphia and being wooed by the man "back home," she returned to Curwensville. However, the call of far-away places led her to leave her hometown for California where she worked for Pacific Mutual and about a year later found her dream job with Trans World Airlines.

On August 26, 1950 **Matilda Kay Thompson** married **Albert R. Brunetti** (born June 12, 1924; d. August 19, 2012; son of Oreste and Edith Durandetto Brunetti). They are the parents of one child, a daughter, Mavis Kim, born on September 2, 1952. Following a divorce from Albert Brunetti, years later on May 22, 1980 Kay married **Robert A. Walker** of Clearfield.

The child of Kay Thompson and Albert Brunetti

Mavis Kim (b. September 2, 1952 in Clearfield) (10ᵗʰ)

10th generation (aligns with that of the John Pifer Paternal Lineage)

Kim Richards lives in Cathedral City, California and is based in Palm Springs where she is a Buyer and Personal Shopper for Macy's. In 1970 Kim married Earl Richards, but the marriage later ended in divorce.

Judith Evelyn

Judith holds an earned doctorate in administration; served as a high school English teacher, principal, and assistant to the superintendent; worked for the Pennsylvania Department of Education; and is the Director of the Capital Area Institute for Mathematics and Science at Penn State Harrisburg. She also heads a private consulting business (Educon) and a publishing company (Yesteryear Publishing). In addition, she has chaired a number of major civic events and is the author of eighteen books, many on social history.

On September 6, 1958 **Judith Evelyn Thompson** (b. March 9, 1937) married **Thomas Eugene Ball** (b. January 31, 1937), son of Elmer and Rena Graham Ball. Following a divorce, on February 25, 1972 Judith married **Walter C. Witmer** (b. January 18, 1931; d. June 13, 2003), son of Miles and Ethel Espenshade Witmer).

The children of Judith Thompson and Thomas Ball

    I.   **Jean Rochelle Ball** (b. March 7, 1959 in Harrisburg) (10th)

    II.   **Thomas Ross Ball** (b. April 23, 1968 in Camp Hill) (10th)

10th generation (aligns with that of the John Pifer Paternal Lineage)

Jean Rochelle Ball Jacobs is the staff accountant for Kurtz Bros. in Clearfield, Pennsylvania. She married James Gary Jacobs (b. October 3, 1948) in 1984.

The children of Jean Rochelle Ball and James Jacobs

    I.   **Jordan Ashlee** (b. April 17, 1986 in Clearfield) (11th)

    II.   **Jillian Rochelle** (b. October 29, 1992 in Clearfield) (11th)

Thomas Ross Ball is the owner of Thomas Ball Entertainment in Hershey, Pennsylvania. He married **Michelle Ann Garger** (b. 1971) in 2000; they were divorced in 2015. The children of Thomas Ross Ball and Michelle Garger

    I.   **Emily Madison** (b. July 11, 2002 in Harrisburg) (11th)

    II.   **Olivia Emerson** (b. June 27, 2005 in Harrisburg) (11th)

11th generation (aligns with that of the John Pifer Paternal Lineage)

As of September 2015:

    Jordan Ashlee Jacobs is employed by Laborers Int'l. Union of North America 158 HCL.

    Jillian Rochelle Jacobs is Hospital Operations Coordinator for United Health Services.

    Emily Madison Ball is in eighth grade at the Lower Dauphin Middle School.

    Olivia Emerson Ball is in fifth grade at Conewago Elementary School.

Jo Ellen

Jo Ellen began her professional career with the Federal Bureau of Investigation (FBI) in Washington, DC, followed by a position with the National Security Agency (the top intelligence organization of the U.S. government), then the newest government agency—later to become the premium agency with the highest clearances required—where she quickly earned a high-level administrative position. She later joined her husband in his business, Lorenz and Lorenz Certified Public Accountants.

On September 6, 1958, in a double wedding ceremony shared with her sister Judith, **Jo Ellen Thompson** (b. November 6, 1938) married **Eugene Kendall Lorenz** (b. September 19, 1932), the son of Alma ("Bonnie") Corinne Miller and Eugene Hurdle Lorenz.

The children of Jo Ellen Thompson and Eugene Kendall Lorenz

    I. **Janelle Corinne Lorenz Wright** (b. January 2, 1969) (10th)

    II. **Eugene Kendall Lorenz, Jr.** (b. April 17, 1970; d. January 3, 2013) (10th)

10th generation (aligns with that of the John Pifer Paternal Lineage)

Janelle Lorenz Wright manages real estate for her parents and her family. Previously, she was employed by KPMG Peat Marwick and as the private label buyer for Saks Fifth Avenue's catalog division.

Janelle Lorenz married **Jay Oscar Wright** (b. December 12, 1969, St. Johnsbury, Vermont) on October 25, 1997. They reside in Potomac, Maryland. They are the parents of

    I. **Corinne Catherine Wright** (b. May 29, 2001 in Sarasota, Florida) (11th)

    II. **Theodore Piers Wright** (b. September 30, 2002 in Silver Spring, Maryland) (11th)

11th generation (aligns with that of the John Pifer Paternal Lineage)

As of September 2015:

    Corinne Catherine Wright is in the ninth grade at The Connelly School of the Holy Child, Potomac, Maryland.

    Theodore Piers Wright is in the sixth grade at Echelon Academy, Sandy Spring, Maryland.

Elizabeth Nan

Nan began her professional career with the National Security Agency in Washington, DC. She later moved to Southern California where she worked for the City of Anaheim. Following a return to Pennsylvania, she worked in Development for Dickinson College in Carlisle before finding her niche in Public Relations for Penn State's College of Medicine and Hershey Medical Center. Currently she manages and is the page designer for Yesteryear Publishing.

On August 18, 1965 **Elizabeth Nan Thompson** (b. August 19, 1942) married **Joel Keith Edmunds** (b. August 14, 1942), the son of Irvin C. and Jaclyn Beck Edmunds.

The children of Elizabeth Nan Thompson and Joel Keith Edmunds

  I. **Shayne Scott Edmunds** (b. December 9, 1965 in Northridge, California) (10th)

  II. **Jesse Joel Edmunds** (b. November 6, 1979 in Lucerne Valley, California) (10th)

10th generation (aligns with that of the John Pifer Paternal Lineage)

Shayne Edmunds married **Ada Grace Graybill** (b. November 10, 1969) on June 15, 1999. They are co-owners of the Neato Burrito restaurant chain located throughout South Central Pennsylvania and reside in Dillsburg, Pennsylvania. They are the parents of

  I. **Aero Graham** (b. April 18, 2004 in Harrisburg, Pennsylvania) (11th)

  II. **Iris Isadora** (b. September 2, 2005 in Harrisburg, Pennsylvania) (11th)

Jesse Edmunds is an outdoor adventurer as well as an accomplished musician who currently performs in the Greater Harrisburg, Pennsylvania area. He resides in Hershey, Pennsylvania.

11th generation (aligns with that of the John Pifer Paternal Lineage)

As of September 2015:

  Aero Graham is in the sixth grade at Northern Middle School in Dillsburg, Pennsylvania.

  Iris Isadora is in the fifth grade at Northern Elementary School in Dillsburg, Pennsylvania.

---

[i] Note the large number of years between the birth dates of (16) Laurence and (17) Laurence, all the more reason to assume there is an unidentified generation here.

[ii] www.avocadoridge.com/carney/getperson.php?personID=12836&tree=tree1&tngprint...

[iii] "Frontier Forts of Pennsylvania," V. II, pp. 241, 244, 284.

[iv] Vol. 5, pp. 653-654.

[v] From *The Story of Kate and* Howard: Nearby Brockwayville was home to various newspapers, one of which was *The Dubois Evening Express,* started in 1883, becoming a daily in 1893; Richard (Dick) Pifer, brother of John Pifer, served a time as editor Another of several newspapers in this small city was *The Morning Herald*, published by Charles J. Bangert and V. King Pifer, a cousin to John Pifer.

[vi] There are inconsistencies throughout with the birth date of John F. Pifer; the memory card at his memorial service gave the birth date as 1886, which is obviously a misprint and was intended to be 1868; Ancestry.com uses 1867.

[vii] It was this gentleman's daughter or perhaps daughter-in-law who sent a note to my mother (who would have been a cousin to Catherine Princetta) of Catherine Princetta's passing. At the time my mother wondered who this Mrs. Bowser was. As I recall, there was no return address, just a postmark on the envelope.

[viii] This dress is framed and still in the possession of the family.

[iv] Mother told us that this is the spelling Howard used and she continued with it.

[x] Howard used the "Jr." designation even though his middle name was not that of his father.

Paternal Lineage

for

Matilda Adeline Smith Pifer

Paternal Lineage for Matilda Adeline Smith Pifer

"The Smiths"

> ### Overview of early ancestors
>
> **William McElhaney,** Donegal, Ireland, is the first ancestor of Matilda Adeline Smith to be identified. No record was found of the names of his parents or of his wife.
>
> William's son is **Andrew McElhaney** (b. 1755 in Donegal, Ireland; d. January 20, 1828) who married **Mary Campbell** (b. 1768; d. 1845).
>
> Andrew and Mary are the parents of three sons and two daughters, born between 1791 and 1811. Their youngest daughter is **Elizabeth Mary McElhaney** (b. 1811; d. 1896). She became the wife of **Robert Harrison Smith** (b. December 29, 1809; d. October 14, 1896).
>
> It could be said that the American lineage of Matilda Adeline Smith begins with Robert Harrison Smith who was born in Donegal, Ireland, and immigrated to America. However, since Robert Harrison Smith's mother (Mary Elizabeth Groves) is known, as are the parents (Andrew and Mary Campbell McElhaney) of Elizabeth Mary McElhaney, **the union of Robert Harrison Smith and Elizabeth May McElhaney will be considered the 3rd generation in the lineage of Matilda Adeline Smith.**

1st generation (aligns with 3rd generation of John Pifer's Paternal Lineage)

William McElhaney (b. 1727; d. 1805), born in Donegal, Ireland, is the father of **Andrew McElhaney** (b. 1755; died January 20, 1828), also born in Donegal, Ireland. (2nd)

2nd generation (aligns with 4th generation of John Pifer Paternal Lineage)

The second generation is the melding of two separate families:

Family #1.
Andrew McElhaney (b. 1755 in Cloonmore, Donegal, Ireland; d. January 20, 1828) married **Mary Campbell** (b. 1768; d. 1845). Andrew and Mary are the parents of three sons and two daughters, born between 1791 and 1811.

     I.   William (b. 1791; d. 1881)

     II.   Nancy A. (b. 1796; d. 1888)

     III.   James (b. 1797; d. 1814)

     IV.   Andrew (b. 1802; d. 1814)

     V.   **Elizabeth Mary McElhaney** (b. 1811; d. 1896) (3rd)

Family #2.

Mary Elizabeth Groves (no dates available), of Donegal, Ireland, married **Robert Smith** (no other information found). Robert Smith and Mary Elizabeth Groves were the parents of three children all born in County Donegal, Ireland.

I.   **Robert Harrison Smith** (b. December 29, 1809; d. October 14, 1896) immigrated to America. (3rd)

II. Ann (1811-1873) married Samuel Logan

III. Rosanna (1814-1874) married James Waterhouse

3rd generation (aligns with 5th generation of the John Pifer Paternal Lineage)

Robert Harrison Smith (b. December. 29, 1809/10; d. October 14, 1896) married **Elizabeth Mary McElhaney** (b. 1811/1820; d. 1896). (The more likely date of birth is 1820 based on the dates when her children were born.)

Robert Harrison Smith and Elizabeth Mary McElhaney were married in Philadelphia in 1836. They are the parents of nine children:

I.   Mary Ann (b. November 2, 1837; d. 1916); married Peter Detwiler in 1852.

II.   Eliza (b. November 18, 1838; d. 1933 [or 1930])

III. **Robert B.** (b. June 20, 1841 in Philadelphia [or Washington Township, Jefferson County]; died in 1916 [or on January 6, 1919] in Jefferson Township) (4th)

IV.   William Hood (b. 1843; d. 1899)

V.   Margaret (b. June 4, 1844; d. 1865)

VI.   Rosanna (b. June 8, 1850; d. 1933); married Andrew Logan (b. 1847)

VII. (Susan) Agnes (b. March 21, 1850; d. 1935) was known as Aunt Agnes to the daughters of her brother Robert B. Agnes died in Cincinnati, Ohio.

VIII. Samuel James, a twin of Susan Agnes (b. March 21, 1850; d. 1932)

IX.   John Wray (b. 1853; d. 1926)

(There must be an error with the date of Rosanna's birth in 1850 and that of her twin siblings, Susan and Samuel, also 1850. I have not been able to find more accurate information.)

(Margaret, Rosanna, and [Susan] Agnes are mentioned in letters written by the children of their brother, Robert B. Smith)

4th generation (aligns with 6th generation of the John Pifer Paternal Lineage [and the 1st generation of Matilda's Maternal Lineage])

Robert B. Smith (b. June 20, 1840/1; d. 1916 [or January 6, 1919] in DuBois) married Mary Ann McElheney (b. 1843 in Portsmouth, Ohio; d. 1882). Robert's date of death is unconfirmed; however, Robert lived well into adulthood as photos in the possession of Judith attest. Very little is known about Mary Ann McElheney other than the dates of birth and death.[i] Mary Ann's death at age 39 was likely the result of complications from childbirth (see birthdate of her youngest child).

Sometime around 1864 Mary Ann McElheney and Robert B. Smith were married and are the parents of one son and seven daughters, five of whom reached adulthood and all of whom were born in Washington Township:

I. Jessie Idora (b. March 23, 1865; d. December 3, 1946)
    Married Jake Heiges
        Children: Robert, Clark, Hilpa, Hazel, Margaret

II. Robert M. (b. 1867) (No trace can be found of Robert, except perhaps a handwritten entry in Matilda's Bible where she likely is referring to her brother, "Dear Rob died July 22, 1941, Los Angeles, CA.")

III. Evelena (Lena, Lennie) (b. 1869)
    Married M. E. Heiges, Jr. and lived in Hubbard, Ohio
        Children: Inez, Margaret Longwell, Helen, and Mary Patterson
        (whose daughter's name is Margaret)

IV. Matilda Adeline (b. June 2, 1872; d. May 1, 1955) (5th)
    Married John F. Pifer
        (see progeny below)

V. Ella W. (b. circa 1874)

VI. Adda (b. circa 1879)

VII. Rosanna (b. June 24, 1880; d. September 11, 1970)
    Married (Michael) Edward Stormer
        Child: Edward, Jr.

VIII. Ella (Nell), listed in family notes as the youngest (b. 1882)
    Married a Mr. Jordan (possibly James B. Jordan on December 22, 1913, but there is no confirmation of his Christian name).

5th generation (aligns with 7th generation of the John Pifer Paternal Lineage [and the 2nd generation of Matilda's Maternal Lineage])

Matilda Adeline Smith (b. June 2, 1872 at Lane's Mills or Beech Woods, Washington Township, Jefferson County; d. May 1, 1955 in Curwensville); married John F. Pifer (b. July 25, 1867/8;[ii] d. May 3, 1954).

Matilda Adeline Smith, wearing the white wedding dress she had hand sewn,[iii] and John F. Pifer were married on June 20, 1894. They are the parents of the following children:

I. Josephine Smith (b. June 14, 1895 in Jefferson County; d. September 23, 1972) married Droz Hamilton (b. 1887; d. 1961) on December 20, 1919

> Noel Franklin (born 1934), living in Reston, Virginia (m. Karin G.)
> > Two adopted children

II. Ruby Idora (b. October 10, 1897 likely in Jefferson County; d. June 14, 1983 in Canton, Ohio); married in Punxsutawney in 1919 to Thomas Jefferson Wayne (b. June 30, 1898 in DuBois; d. August 13. 1975 in Ohio)

> John A. (b. April 18, 1924; d. March 25, 1994) (m. Nanette)
> > Gregory
> > Lisa

> Thomas J. (b. June 20, 1929; d. August 16, 1977)
> > Thomas
> > Mark

III. Jessie Beverly (b. July 9, 1905 in Brockway; d. June 1, 1993 in Hershey); married Harry Hawes on March 21, 1930 and later married John Mohney on June 22, 1963

IV. **Katherine Shields** (b. February 11, 1908 in Curwensville; d. January 31, 1998 in Hummelstown/Hershey) (6th)
> (see progeny below)

V. Margaret Jean (b. February 11, 1910 in Curwensville; d. December 30, 1958 in Clearfield); married A. Chester Bloom (b. December 12, 1908; d. November 13, 1993) in 1927.

> Chester Eugene (b. 1927) (m. Mable Riddle)
> > Mark
> > Debbie

> Donald Dwight (b. 1929) (m. Kathryn Lorraine Valimont)

> Janet Lynn (b. December 15, 1946), lives in Stafford, MO; m. James C. Carter)
> > Shelly

6th generation (aligns with 8th generation of the John Pifer Paternal Lineage [and the 3rd generation of Matilda's Maternal Lineage])

Kathryn Shields Pifer (b. February 11, 1908; died January 31, 1998) married **Howard V. Thompson** (b. April 10, 1904 in Clearfield; died January 14, 1964 in Clearfield).

Catherine S. Pifer (as her name appears on the marriage license)[iv] and Howard V. Thompson, Jr.[v] were married on June 20, 1927 in Clearfield; the date was the 33rd wedding anniversary of her parents' marriage. Catherine and Howard are the parents of the following children:

    I.   **Matilda Kay** (b. November 1, 1930 in Curwensville) (7th)

    II.   **Judith Evelyn** (b. March 9, 1937 in Clearfield) (7th)

    III.   **Jo Ellen** (b. November 6, 1938 in Clearfield) (7th)

    IV.   **Elizabeth Nan** (b. August 19, 1942 in Clearfield) (7th)

7th generation (aligns with 9th generation of the John Pifer Paternal Lineage [and the 4th generation of Matilda's Maternal Lineage])

It was this generation who moved from Curwensville, each in turn after high school graduation: Kay moving to California, but returning to Curwensville in the late 1980s; Judith settling in Hummelstown, Pennsylvania to teach in the newly formed Lower Dauphin Junior-Senior High School; Jo Ellen leaving for government service and later working in her husband's CPA firm in the DC area; and Nan to DC, then California, returning to live in Hershey, Pennsylvania, where she worked in public relations and publications for the Penn State College of Medicine and Hershey Medical Center, now as designer for Yesteryear Publishing.

At this point the genealogies merge and become one with the Thompson Sisters who originate through the marriage of Catherine Pifer and Howard V. Thompson.

As explained in the section on the Paternal Lineage of John Frederick Pifer, which was used as the baseline, the genealogies are aligned by the ages of those who lived at a common time. Because a lineage begins with the first generation of a family that could be found, a person identified in the third generation of one lineage might match in age to those in the sixth generation of another's lineage. For example, in this set of genealogies, persons named in the seventh generation of Elizabeth's Paternal Lineage, would match in age with those in the eighth generation of John Pifer's Maternal Lineage as well as in his Paternal Lineage because his ancestors on both sides (mother and father) are of the same timeframe (similar birth dates).

Most frequently a person appears in different generations in the separate lineages. For example, because Matilda Pifer's mother's lineage could not be traced back very many generations (There are no records for the key people), Catherine and Howard Thompson are only the third generation in her Maternal Lineage, but are **eighth** in John Pifer's Maternal Lineage—or even **27th** if we count the lineage back to William the Conqueror.

To demonstrate, those of the **1ˢᵗ generation** of Matilda Smith Pifer's **Maternal Lineage** would align with the following:

- **4th generation** of her own **Paternal Lineage**

- **4th generation** of H. J. Thompson's **Paternal Lineage**

- **5th generation** of Elizabeth Spencer Thompson's **Paternal Lineage**

- **6th generation** of Elizabeth's **Maternal Lineage** and of H. J.'s **Maternal Lineage**

- **6th generation** of John F. Pifer's **Maternal Lineage** and **Paternal Lineage** beginning in America or the 25th generation (if we include to William the Conqueror) of his **Maternal Lineage**

THE THOMPSON SISTERS ARE

9th generation of Howard Jefferson Thompson's Maternal Lineage
7th generation of his Paternal Lineage

9th generation of Elizabeth Spencer Thompson's Maternal Lineage
8th generation of her Paternal Lineage

9th (or 28th if we include back to William the Conqueror) generation of John Frederick Pifer's Maternal Lineage
9th generation of his Paternal Lineage

4th generation of Matilda Smith Pifer's Maternal Lineage
7th generation of her Paternal Lineage

Matilda Kay

Following graduation Kay, a talented dancer, went to Philadelphia and auditioned for a place in a music hall/theatre chorus line. After a year in Philadelphia and being wooed by the man "back home," she returned to Curwensville. However, the call of far-away places led her to leave her hometown for California where she worked for Pacific Mutual and about a year later found her dream job with Trans World Airlines.

On August 26, 1950 **Matilda Kay Thompson** married **Albert R. Brunetti** (born June 12, 1924; d. August 19, 2012; son of Oreste and Edith Durandetto Brunetti). They are the parents of one child, a daughter, Mavis Kim, born on September 2, 1952. Following a divorce from Albert Brunetti, years later on May 22, 1980 Kay married **Robert A. Walker** of Clearfield.

The child of Kay Thompson and Albert Brunetti

Mavis Kim (b. September 2, 1952 in Clearfield) (8ᵗʰ)

8th generation (aligns with the 10th generation of the John Pifer Paternal Lineage [and the 5th generation of Matilda's Maternal Lineage])

Kim Richards lives in Cathedral City, California and is based in Palm Springs where she is a Buyer and Personal Shopper for Macy's. In 1970 Kim married Earl Richards, but the marriage later ended in divorce.

Judith Evelyn

Judith holds an earned doctorate in administration; served as a high school English teacher, teacher, principal, and assistant to the superintendent; worked for the Pennsylvania Department of Education; and is the Director of the Capital Area Institute for Mathematics and Science at Penn State Harrisburg. She also heads a private consulting business (Educon) and a publishing company (Yesteryear Publishing). In addition, she has chaired a number of major civic events and is the author of eighteen books, many on social history.

On September 6, 1958 **Judith Evelyn Thompson** (b. March 9, 1937) married **Thomas Eugene Ball** (b. January 31, 1937), son of Elmer and Rena Graham Ball. Following a divorce, on February 25, 1972 Judith married **Walter C. Witmer** (b. January 18, 1931; d. June 13, 2003), son of Miles and Ethel Espenshade Witmer).

The children of Judith Evelyn Thompson and Thomas Eugene Ball

- I.   **Jean Rochelle** (b. March 7, 1959 in Harrisburg) (8th)
- II. **Thomas Ross** (b. April 23, 1968 in Camp Hill) (8th)

8th generation (aligns with the 10th generation of the John Pifer Paternal Lineage [and the 5th generation of Matilda's Maternal Lineage])

Jean Rochelle Ball Jacobs is the staff accountant for Kurtz Bros. in Clearfield, Pennsylvania. She married **James Gary Jacobs** (b. October 3, 1948) in 1984.

The children of Jean Rochelle Ball and James Jacobs

- I.   **Jordan Ashlee** (b. April 17, 1986 in Clearfield) (9th)
- II. **Jillian Rochelle** (b. October 29, 1992 in Clearfield) (9th)

Thomas Ross Ball is the owner of Thomas Ball Entertainment in Hershey, Pennsylvania. He married **Michelle Ann Garger** (b. 1971) in 2000; they were divorced in 2015.

The children of Thomas Ross Ball and Michelle Garger

- I.   **Emily Madison** (b. July 11, 2002 in Harrisburg) (9th)
- II. **Olivia Emerson** (b. June 27, 2005 in Harrisburg) (9th)

9th generation (aligns with the 11th generation of the John Pifer Paternal Lineage [and the 6th generation of Matilda's Maternal Lineage])

As of September 2015:

>**Jordan Ashlee Jacobs** is employed by Laborers Int'l. Union of North America 158 HCL.
>
>**Jillian Rochelle Jacobs** is Hospital Operations Coordinator for United Health Services.
>
>**Emily Madison Ball** is in eighth grade at the Lower Dauphin Middle School.
>
>**Olivia Emerson Ball** is in fifth grade at Conewago Elementary School.

Jo Ellen

Jo Ellen began her professional career with the Federal Bureau of Investigation (FBI) in Washington, DC, followed by a position with the National Security Agency (the top intelligence organization of the U.S. government), then the newest government agency—later to become the premium agency with the highest clearances required—where she quickly earned a high-level administrative position. She later joined her husband in his business, Lorenz and Lorenz Certified Public Accountants.

On September 6, 1958, **Jo Ellen Thompson** (b. November 6, 1938) married **Eugene Kendall Lorenz** (b. September 19, 1932), the son of Alma ("Bonnie") Corinne Miller and Eugene Hurdle Lorenz.

The children of Jo Ellen Thompson and Eugene Kendall Lorenz

>I.   **Janelle Corinne Lorenz Wright** (b. January 2, 1969) (8th)
>
>II. **Eugene Kendall Lorenz, Jr.** (b. April 17, 1970; d. January 3, 2013) (8th)

8th generation (aligns with the 10th generation of the John Pifer Paternal Lineage [and the 5th generation of Matilda's Maternal Lineage])

Janelle Lorenz Wright manages real estate for her parents and her family. Previously, she was employed by KPMG Peat Marwick and as the private label buyer for Saks Fifth Avenue's catalog division.

Janelle Lorenz married **Jay Oscar Wright** (b. December 12, 1969, St. Johnsbury, Vermont) on October 25, 1997. They reside in Potomac, Maryland. They are the parents of

>I.   **Corinne Catherine Wright** (b. May 29, 2001 in Sarasota, Florida) (9th)
>
>II. **Theodore Piers Wright** (b. September 30, 2002 in Silver Spring, Maryland) (9th)

9th generation (aligns with the 11th generation of the John Pifer Paternal Lineage [and the 6th generation of Matilda's Maternal Lineage])

As of September 2015:

>**Corinne Catherine Wright** is in the ninth grade at The Connelly School of the Holy Child, Potomac, Maryland.
>
>**Theodore Piers Wright** is in the sixth grade at Echelon Academy, Sandy Spring, Maryland.

Elizabeth Nan

Nan began her professional career with the National Security Agency in Washington, DC. She later moved to Southern California where she worked for the City of Anaheim. Following a return to Pennsylvania, she worked in Development for Dickinson College in Carlisle before finding her niche in Public Relations for Penn State's College of Medicine and Hershey Medical Center. Currently she manages and is the page designer for Yesteryear Publishing.

On August 18, 1965 Elizabeth Nan Thompson (b. August 19, 1942) married Joel Keith Edmunds (b. August 14, 1942), the son of Irvin C. and Jaclyn Beck Edmunds.

The children of Elizabeth Nan Thompson and Joel Keith Edmunds

    I.   Shayne Scott Edmunds (b. December 9, 1965 in Northridge, California) (8th)

    II. Jesse Joel Edmunds (b. November 6, 1979 in Lucerne Valley, California) (8th)

8th generation (aligns with the 10th generation of the John Pifer Paternal Lineage [and the 5th generation of Matilda's Maternal Lineage])

Shayne Edmunds and his wife, Grace Graybill, are co-owners of the Neato Burrito restaurant chain located throughout South Central Pennsylvania.

Shayne Edmunds married Ada Grace Graybill (b. November 10, 1969) on June 15, 1999. They reside in Dillsburg, Pennsylvania and are the parents of

    I.   Aero Graham (b. April 18, 2004 in Harrisburg, Pennsylvania) (9th)

    II. Iris Isadora (b. September 2, 2005 in Harrisburg, Pennsylvania) (9th)

Jesse Edmunds is an outdoor adventurer as well as an accomplished musician who currently performs in the Greater Harrisburg, Pennsylvania area. He resides in Hershey, Pennsylvania.

9th generation (aligns with the 11th generation of the John Pifer Paternal Lineage [and the 6th generation of Matilda's Maternal Lineage])

As of September 2015:

    Aero Graham is in the sixth grade at Northern Middle School in Dillsburg, Pennsylvania.

    Iris Isadora is in the fifth grade at Northern Elementary School in Dillsburg, Pennsylvania.

---

[i]   There is a strong possibility that she was born in Portsmouth, Ohio.

[ii]   There are inconsistencies throughout with the birth date of John F. Pifer; the memory card at his memorial service gave the birth date as 1886, which is obviously a misprint and was intended to be 1868; Ancestry.com uses 1867.

[iii] Still in the possession of the family (framed).

[iv] Mother told us that this is the spelling Howard used and she continued with it.

[v]   Howard used the "Jr." designation even though his middle name was not that of his father.

Maternal Lineage

for

Matilda Adeline Smith Pifer

Maternal Lineage for Matilda Adeline Smith Pifer

"Mary Ann McElheny"

The maternal lineage for Matilda Adeline Smith begins and ends with her mother, **Mary Ann McElheney**, who was born in 1843 in Ohio. **There is no record of the parents or other ancestors of Mary Ann McElheney** (unless what is noted below as a supposition is, in fact, actual).

It would be interesting to think that **Mary Ann McElheney** was in some way related to her husband's mother, **Elizabeth Mary McElheney** who became the wife of **Robert Harrison Smith.** Elizabeth Mary McElheney and Robert Harrison Smith then became the parents of Robert B. Smith whom Mary Ann McElheney married. In other words, **Robert B. Smith,** *the son of Elizabeth Mary* **McElheney, married Mary Ann McElheney,** but we know of no substantiated familial relationship here.

Mary Ann McElheney married Robert B. Smith (b. June 20, 1841; his date of death is unconfirmed, but thought to be 1916 [or January 6, 1919]). However, Robert lived well into adulthood attested to by photos in the possession of the family.

1st generation of record (aligns with the 6th generation of the John Pifer Paternal Lineage)

Mary Ann McElheney (b. 1843; d. 1882)

Very little personal information is known about Mary Ann McElheney other than the dates of birth and death.[i] Her parents' names are unknown as of this writing.

Mary Ann McElheney (b. 1843; d. 1882) married **Robert B. Smith** (b. June 20, 1840/1; d. 1916 [or January 6, 1919] in DuBois). Robert's date of death is unconfirmed; however, Robert lived well into adulthood as photos in the possession of Judith attest. Mary Ann's death at age 39 was likely the result of complications from childbirth (see birth date of her youngest child).

Mary Ann McElheney and Robert B. Smith were married sometime in 1864. They had one son and seven daughters, all of whom were born in Washington Township and five of whom reached adulthood:

> I.   Jessie Idora (b. March 23, 1865; d. December 3, 1946)
> Married Jake Heiges
>> Children: Robert, Clark, Hilpa, Hazel, Margaret
>
> II.   Robert M. (b. 1867) (No trace can be found of Robert, except perhaps a handwritten entry in Matilda's Bible where she likely is referring to her brother, "Dear Rob died July 22, 1941, Los Angeles, CA.")

III.   Evelena (Lena, Lennie) (b. 1869)
        Married M. E. Heiges, Jr. and lived in Hubbard, Ohio
            Children: Inez, Margaret Longwell, Helen, and Mary Patterson
                (whose daughter's name is Margaret)

IV.   **Matilda Adeline** (b. June 2, 1872; d. May 1, 1955) **(2ⁿᵈ)**
        Married John F. Pifer
            (see progeny below)

V.   Ella W. (b. circa 1874) (may be in error)

VI.   Adda (b. circa 1879)

VII.   Rosanna (b. June 24, 1880; d. September 11, 1970)
        Married (Michael) Edward Stormer
            Child: Edward, Jr.

VIII.   Ella W. (Nell), listed in family notes as the youngest (b. 1882)
        Married James B. Jordan on December 22, 1913, but there is no confirmation
        that this is the Ella we are seeking.

2ⁿᵈ generation (aligns with the 7ᵗʰ generation of the John Pifer Paternal Lineage)

Matilda Adeline Smith (b. June 2, 1872; d. May 1, 1955) born at Lane's Mills or Beech Woods, Washington Township, Jefferson County and died in Curwensville; married **John F. Pifer** (b. July 25, 1867/8;[ii] d. May 3, 1954).

Matilda Adeline Smith, wearing the white wedding dress she had hand sewn,[iii] and John F. Pifer were married on June 20, 1894. They are the parents of the following children:

I.   Josephine Smith (b. June 14, 1895 in Jefferson County; d. September 23, 1972);
        married Droz Hamilton (b. 1887; d. 1961) on December 20, 1919

            Noel Franklin (born 1934), living in Reston, Virginia (m. Karin G.)
                Two adopted children

II.   Ruby Idora (b. October 10, 1897 likely in Jefferson County; d. June 14, 1983 in
        Canton, Ohio); married in Punxsutawney in 1919 to Thomas Jefferson Wayne
        (b. June 30, 1898 in DuBois; d. August 13. 1975 in Ohio)

            John A. (b. April 18, 1924; d. March 25, 1994) (m. Nanette)
                Gregory
                Lisa

            Thomas J. (b. June 20, 1929; d. August 16, 1977)
                Thomas
                Mark

III.   Jessie Beverly (b. July 9, 1905 in Brockway; d. June 1, 1993 in Hershey); married
        Harry Hawes on March 21, 1930 and later married John Mohney on June 22, 1963

IV.   **Katherine Shields** (b. February 11, 1908 in Curwensville; d. January 31, 1998 in Hummelstown/Hershey) **(3rd)**
(see progeny below)

V.   Margaret Jean (b. February 11, 1910 in Curwensville; d. December 30, 1958 in Clearfield); married A. Chester Bloom (b. December 12, 1908; d. November 13, 1993) in 1927.
       Chester Eugene (b. 1927) (m. Mable Riddle)
            Mark
            Debbie
       Donald Dwight (b. 1929) (m. Kathryn Lorraine Valimont)
       Janet Lynn (b. December 15, 1946), lives in Stafford, MO; m. James C. Carter)
            Shelly

3rd generation (aligns with 8th generation of the John Pifer Paternal Lineage)

Kathryn Shields Pifer (b. February 11, 1908; died January 31, 1998) married **Howard V. Thompson** (b. April 10, 1904 in Clearfield; died January 14, 1964 in Clearfield).

Catherine S. Pifer (as her name appears on the marriage license)[iv] and Howard V. Thompson, Jr.[v] were married on June 20, 1927 in Clearfield; the date was the 33rd wedding anniversary of her parents' marriage. Catherine and Howard are the parents of the following children:

I.   **Matilda Kay** (b. November 1, 1930 in Curwensville) **(4th)**

II.   **Judith Evelyn** (b. March 9, 1937 in Clearfield) **(4th)**

III. **Jo Ellen** (b. November 6, 1938 in Clearfield) **(4th)**

IV.   **Elizabeth Nan** (b. August 19, 1942 in Clearfield) **(4th)**

4th generation (aligns with 9th generation of the John Pifer Paternal Lineage)

It was this generation who moved from Curwensville, each in turn after high school graduation: Kay moving to California, but returning to Curwensville in the late 1980s; Judith settling in Hummelstown, Pennsylvania to teach in the newly formed Lower Dauphin Junior-Senior High School; Jo Ellen leaving for government service and later working in her husband's CPA firm in the DC area; and Nan to DC, then California, returning to live in Hershey, Pennsylvania, where she worked in public relations and publications for the Penn State College of Medicine and Hershey Medical Center, now as designer for Yesteryear Publishing.

At this point the genealogies merge and become one with the Thompson Sisters who originate through the marriage of Catherine Pifer and Howard V. Thompson.

As explained in the section on the Paternal Lineage of John Frederick Pifer, which was used as the baseline, the genealogies are aligned by the ages of those who lived at a common time. Because a lineage begins with the first generation of a family that could be found, a person identified in the third generation of one lineage might match in age to those in the sixth generation of another's lineage. For example, in this set of genealogies, persons named in the seventh generation of Elizabeth's Paternal Lineage, would match in age with those in the eighth generation of John Pifer's Maternal Lineage as well as in his Paternal Lineage because his ancestors on both sides (mother and father) are of the same timeframe (similar birth dates).

Most frequently a person appears in different generations in the separate lineages. For example, because Matilda Pifer's mother's lineage could not be traced back very many generations (There are no records for the key people), Catherine and Howard Thompson are only the third generation in her Maternal Lineage, but are eighth in John Pifer's Maternal Lineage—or even 27th if we count the lineage back to William the Conqueror.

To demonstrate, those of the 1st generation of Matilda Smith Pifer's Maternal Lineage would align with the following:

- 4th generation of her own Paternal Lineage

- 4th generation of H. J. Thompson's Paternal Lineage

- 5th generation of Elizabeth Spencer Thompson's Paternal Lineage

- 6th generation of Elizabeth's Maternal Lineage and of H. J.'s Maternal Lineage

- 6th generation of John F. Pifer's Maternal Lineage and Paternal Lineage beginning in America or the 25th generation (if we include to William the Conqueror) of his Maternal Lineage

THE THOMPSON SISTERS ARE

9th generation of Howard Jefferson Thompson's Maternal Lineage
7th generation of his Paternal Lineage

9th generation of Elizabeth Spencer Thompson's Maternal Lineage
8th generation of her Paternal Lineage

9th (or 28th if we include back to William the Conqueror) generation of John Frederick Pifer's Maternal Lineage
9th generation of his Paternal Lineage

4th generation of Matilda Smith Pifer's Maternal Lineage
7th generation of her Paternal Lineage

Matilda Kay

Following graduation Kay, a talented dancer, went to Philadelphia and auditioned for a place in a music hall/theatre chorus line. After a year in Philadelphia and being wooed by the man "back home," she returned to Curwensville. However, the call of far-away places led her to leave her hometown for California where she worked for Pacific Mutual and about a year later found her dream job with Trans World Airlines.

On August 26, 1950 Matilda Kay Thompson married Albert R. Brunetti (born June 12, 1924; d. August 19, 2012; son of Oreste and Edith Durandetto Brunetti). They are the parents of one child, a daughter, Mavis Kim, born on September 2, 1952. Following a divorce from Albert Brunetti, years later on May 22, 1980 Kay married Robert A. Walker of Clearfield.

The child of Kay Thompson and Albert Brunetti

Mavis Kim (b. September 2, 1952 in Clearfield) (5th)

5th generation (aligns with 10th generation of the John Pifer Paternal Lineage)

Kim Richards lives in Cathedral City, California and is based in Palm Springs where she is a Buyer and Personal Shopper for Macy's. In 1970 Kim married Earl Richards, but the marriage later ended in divorce.

Judith Evelyn

Judith holds an earned doctorate in administration; served as a high school English teacher, teacher, principal, and assistant to the superintendent; worked for the Pennsylvania Department of Education; and is the Director of the Capital Area Institute for Mathematics and Science at Penn State Harrisburg. She also heads a private consulting business (Educon) and a publishing company (Yesteryear Publishing). In addition, she has chaired a number of major civic events and is the author of eighteen books, many on social history.

On September 6, 1958 Judith Evelyn Thompson (b. March 9, 1937) married Thomas Eugene Ball (b. January 31, 1937), son of Elmer and Rena Graham Ball. Following a divorce, on February 25, 1972 Judith married Walter C. Witmer (b. January 18, 1931; d. June 13, 2003), son of Miles and Ethel Espenshade Witmer).

The children of Judith Evelyn Thompson and Thomas Eugene Ball

I.   Jean Rochelle (b. March 7, 1959 in Harrisburg) (5th)

II.   Thomas Ross (b. April 23, 1968 in Camp Hill) (5th)

5th generation (aligns with 10th generation of the John Pifer Paternal Lineage)

Jean Rochelle Ball Jacobs is the staff accountant for Kurtz Bros. in Clearfield, Pennsylvania. She married James Gary Jacobs (b. October 3, 1948) in 1984.

The children of Jean Rochelle Ball and James Jacobs

    I.   **Jordan Ashlee** (b. April 17, 1986 in Clearfield) (6th)

    II.   **Jillian Rochelle** (b. October 29, 1992 in Clearfield) (6th)

Thomas Ross Ball is the owner of Thomas Ball Entertainment in Hershey, Pennsylvania. He married **Michelle Ann Garger** (b. 1971) in 2000; they were divorced in 2015.

The children of Thomas Ross Ball and Michelle Garger

    I.   **Emily Madison** (b. July 11, 2002 in Harrisburg) (6th)

    II.   **Olivia Emerson** (b. June 27, 2005 in Harrisburg) (6th)

6th generation (aligns with 11th generation of the John Pifer Paternal Lineage)

As of September 2015:

Jordan Ashlee Jacobs is employed by Laborers Int'l. Union of North America 158 HCL.

Jillian Rochelle Jacobs is Hospital Operations Coordinator for United Health Services.

Emily Madison Ball is in eighth grade at the Lower Dauphin Middle School.

Olivia Emerson Ball is in fifth grade at Conewago Elementary School.

Jo Ellen

Jo Ellen began her professional career with the Federal Bureau of Investigation (FBI) in Washington, DC, followed by a position with the National Security Agency (the top intelligence organization of the U.S. government), then the newest government agency—later to become the premium agency with the highest clearances required—where she quickly earned a high-level administrative position. She later joined her husband in his business, Lorenz and Lorenz Certified Public Accountants.

On September 6, 1958, in a double wedding ceremony shared with her sister Judith, **Jo Ellen Thompson** (b. November 6, 1938) married **Eugene Kendall Lorenz** (b. September 19, 1932), the son of Alma ("Bonnie") Corinne Miller and Eugene Hurdle Lorenz.

The children of Jo Ellen Thompson and Eugene Kendall Lorenz

    I. **Janelle Corinne Lorenz Wright** (b. January 2, 1969) (5th)

    II. **Eugene Kendall Lorenz, Jr.** (b. April 17, 1970; d. January 3, 2013) (5th)

5th generation (aligns with 10th generation of the John Pifer Paternal Lineage)

Janelle Lorenz Wright manages real estate for her parents and her family. Previously, she was employed by KPMG Peat Marwick and as the private label buyer for Saks Fifth Avenue's catalog division.

Janelle Lorenz married Jay Oscar Wright (b. December 12, 1969, St. Johnsbury, Vermont) on October 25, 1997. They reside in Potomac, Maryland. They are the parents of

    I.   Corinne Catherine Wright (b. May 29, 2001 in Sarasota, Florida) (6th)

    II.   Theodore Piers Wright (b. September 30, 2002 in Silver Spring, Maryland) (6th)

6th generation (aligns with 11th generation of the John Pifer Paternal Lineage)

As of September 2015:

    Corinne Catherine Wright is in the ninth grade at The Connelly School of the Holy Child, Potomac, Maryland.

    Theodore Piers Wright is in the sixth grade at Echelon Academy, Sandy Spring, Maryland.

Elizabeth Nan

Nan began her professional career with the National Security Agency in Washington, DC. She later moved to Southern California where she worked for the City of Anaheim. Following a return to Pennsylvania, she worked in Development for Dickinson College in Carlisle before finding her niche in Public Relations for Penn State's College of Medicine and Hershey Medical Center. Currently she manages and is the page designer for Yesteryear Publishing.

On August 18, 1965 Elizabeth Nan Thompson (b. August 19, 1942) married Joel Keith Edmunds (b. August 14, 1942), the son of Irvin C. and Jaclyn Beck Edmunds.

The children of Elizabeth Nan Thompson and Joel Keith Edmunds

    I.   Shayne Scott Edmunds (b. December 9, 1965 in Northridge, California) (5th)

    II.   Jesse Joel Edmunds (b. November 6, 1979 in Lucerne Valley, California) (5th)

5th generation (aligns with 10th generation of the John Pifer Paternal Lineage)

Shayne Edmunds and his wife, Grace Graybill, are co-owners of the Neato Burrito restaurant chain located throughout South Central Pennsylvania.

Shayne Edmunds married Ada Grace Graybill (b. November 10, 1969) on June 15, 1999. They reside in Dillsburg, Pennsylvania and are the parents of

    I.   Aero Graham (b. April 18, 2004 in Harrisburg, Pennsylvania) (6th)

    II.   Iris Isadora (b. September 2, 2005 in Harrisburg, Pennsylvania) (6th)

Jesse Edmunds is an outdoor adventurer as well as an accomplished musician who currently performs in the Greater Harrisburg, Pennsylvania area. He resides in Hershey, Pennsylvania.

6th generation (aligns with 11th generation of the John Pifer Paternal Lineage)

As of September 2015:

> **Aero Graham** is in the sixth grade at Northern Middle School in Dillsburg, Pennsylvania.
>
> **Iris Isadora** is in the fifth grade at Northern Elementary School in Dillsburg, Pennsylvania.

---

[i]   There is a strong possibility that she was born in Portsmouth, Ohio which might explain why no records of family can be identified by searching in Jefferson and surrounding Counties.

[ii] There are inconsistencies throughout with the birth date of John F. Pifer; the memory card at his memorial service gave the birth date as 1886, which is obviously a misprint and was intended to be 1868; Ancestry.com uses 1867.

[iii] Still in the possession of the family (framed).

[iv] Mother told us that this is the spelling Howard used and she continued with it.

[v]   Howard used the "Jr." designation even though his middle name was not that of his father.

Paternal Lineage

for

Howard Jefferson Thompson

Paternal Lineage for Howard Jefferson Thompson

"The Thompsons"

Peter Thompson (possible date of birth is February 5, 1764), the first in this lineage to be identified, came to Pennsylvania from Ireland prior to the Revolutionary War and it is believed that he served in the Fifth Pennsylvania Regiment in the American Revolution. Mention is made of Peter Thompson on a return of recruits enlisted for the Fifth Pennsylvania Regiment in Philadelphia. He was discharged in April 1783 at which time he likely was married. He then settled in that part of Bedford County which became Huntingdon County. A news clipping from "The County Review" (submitted by Lenore Wright Davidson of Curwensville to Ancestry.com) notes that Peter "raised a large family about which the Clearfield family knows but little."

> It is also remotely possible that this progenitor was a Peter Thompson [b. 1748; d. March 13, 1811], born in Ireland, who went to Carroll, Maryland, then settled in Huntingdon County; this Peter Thompson is said to have married Mary Patterson [b. in Huntingdon in 1754; d. 1795].

1st generation (dates align with the 3rd generation of the John Pifer Paternal Lineage)

Peter Thompson (b. circa February 1764) is the father of **Ignatius Thompson** (b. September 26, 1784 in Huntingdon County; d. April 26 or May 27, 1861) **(2nd)**

2nd generation (dates align with the 4th generation of the John Pifer Paternal Lineage)

Ignatius Thompson would have been a young man when he traveled with his family to Clearfield County about 1810, "settling on 'The Ridges'" presumably in and above Curwensville where many sections of the area bear the name "Ridge," as in "Ridge Avenue" or "Chestnut Ridge." He then purchased land in upper Lawrence Township, where Glen Richey now stands. It is reported that the family traveled by ox cart, cutting their way through the woods at many points and that "the pioneer unloaded his goods under a large hemlock tree and there made his home until the cabin they were to occupy was completed." (This description is from the clipping contributed by Lenore Wright Davidson to Ancestry.com.)

His disposition was described as "cheerful—with a kindly humor, childlike with a humble opinion of himself." He later served three years as a County Commissioner. His obituary gives the cause of death at 77 as apoplexy, "having had previous attacks of that disease of which he died." (Obituary found in Ancestry.com)

Ignatius Thompson (b. September 26, 1784 in Huntingdon County; d. April 28, 1861) married **Mary Norris** (b. July 30, 1787 in Huntingdon County; d. September 15, 1872 in Glen Ritchey, Clearfield County). Mary was the daughter of John Davis Norris (b. 1765; d. 1838) and Ann Thompson (b.

1767; d. 1840) and a sister of Moses Norris, the progenitor of the Norris families of Clearfield County. Ignatius and Mary Thompson cleared their farm (later to belong to Hazel Owens) and reared three sons and five daughters.

Ignatius Thompson and Mary Norris were married in 1808 and are the parents of the following children:

I.   Nancy Ann (b. 1809) married Joseph Straw (10-11 children)[i]

II.   Mary (b. 1811) married Ross Reed (7 children)

III.   John D. (b. 1813; d. 1886); married Sara Hartsock in 1837) (10 children)

IV.   **James** (b. October 12, 1815 in Glen Richey; d. 1887) (3rd)

V.   Elizabeth (b. 1820) married Elisha Ardery (4 children)

VI.   Esther married R. D. Cummings (1 child)

VII.   A fifth daughter (unknown name) never married

VIII. Josiah (b. 1825; d. 1900); first married Ann Eliza Wilson with whom he had 11 children. After the death of his wife he married Mrs. Susannah Kaufman. His farm, on Hogback Road, was described as "a fine and valuable property." (Ancestry.com)

3rd generation (dates align with the 5th generation of the John Pifer Paternal Lineage)

John D. (the first son of Ignatius and Mary) remained on the homestead and at 18 learned the blacksmith trade. He married in 1837 when he and his wife moved to Curwensville and he continued as a smith for 40 years and, with his brother, entered the foundry business. In 1861 he was elected Associate County Judge, an office he held for five years; he then served as a County Commissioner for three years and ten years as a Justice of the Peace. During the Civil War he was a member of the Board of Relief.

James Thompson (b. October 12, 1815; d. 1887) married **Catherine Hepburn** (b. March 7, 1824; d. 1925, later honored as a Centenarian). Catherine was a daughter of William Hepburn (d. 1858), a native of Scotland. In 1848 the Thompsons moved to Curwensville where James established a foundry with his older brother John. James and Catherine built their home there in 1852. A Democrat, James never sought an office.

James Thompson and Catherine Hepburn married in 1843 and were said to be the parents of ten children (although the names of 11 progeny were identified)

I.   Martha (b. February 11, 1844)

II.   **Francis Ignatius** (b. June 2, 1846; d. 1909) (4th)

III.   William H. (b. February 14, 1848)

IV.   Samantha (b. November 12, 1850)

V.   Mary Alice (b. March 12, 1853)

VI.   Josephine Blanche (b. June 1, 1855; d. March 14, 1925)

VII.   Henrietta (b. November 7, 1856)[ii]

VIII. Leonora (b. November 15, 1858)

IX.   Frances (b. May 12, 1861)

X.   Nannie (b. November 17, 1862)

XI.   Jack (b. April 9, 1865)

4th generation (dates align with the 6th generation of the John Pifer Paternal Lineage)

Francis Ignatius (b. June 2, 1846; d. 1909[iii]) married **Mary Erie Bell** (b. August 15, 1850; d. March 10, 1892), who was the daughter of David Roll Bell (b. February 11, 1824; d. December 31, 1875) and Margery Hoover (b. July 30, 1826; d. December 22, 1892) of Greenwood Township. David and Margery were married in 1844. David Roll Bell was the son of Greenwood Bell [b. November 20, 1785; d. September 8, 1860] and Elizabeth Roll [b. November 14, 1787; d. May 15, 1850], both also of Greenwood Township which possibly was named for him or an earlier relative.

Francis Ignatius, known as Ignatius, was the eldest son of James Thompson. Ignatius assisted his father James and uncle (John Thompson) in their foundry which manufactured ploughs, stoves, and other items needed by a burgeoning community. Ignatius, whose nickname was "Nace," also engaged to a large extent in the lumber business. In 1890 he purchased the budding Anderson Creek Electric Company where his sons "learned the business." Nace later sold this direct current plant to Wm. F. Patton.

Nace was one of the leading Democrats during his life and served as Constable of Curwensville Borough for many years. His son Howard J. tells the story that he and his brothers were roused from their beds some nights because their father, as Constable, was paid $1. per night for lodging arrestees in his home; there were no beds in the jail.

Mary Erie Bell and Francis Ignatius Thompson, married on August 6, 1871, are the parents of the following:

I.   Erie (b. January 28, 1872; d. February 19, 1872[iv])

II.   Walter B. (possibly Bell; b. January 1874; d. February 14, 1946) He first married Edna M. Thompson (although this may not be her maiden name; b. March 1881) in 1900. He later married Charlotte Decker (b. 1890; d. October 1968), daughter of Mary Henderson and David Bell (some sources suggest Charlotte's full name was Charlotte Decker Bell). Walter and Charlotte were married on December 28, 1910 when he was 36 and she was 20; they are the parents of one daughter, Irene, born in 1912. Walter and Charlotte are interred in the Greenlawn Cemetery in Salem, Massachusetts.[v]

III. **Howard Jefferson** (b. January 12, 1878; d. January 3, 1968), whose middle name was chosen to honor the name of both his father and his mother's brother, Jefferson, (7th)

IV.   Maud A. (b. June 10, 1884; d. September 30, 1958) married Clinton Davidson (b.

1882); was widowed, then lived with a Mr. Stamp in Buffalo, NY. (We were told Aunt Maud kept house for Mr. Stamp.) Her family honored her wishes to be interred in her family's section of Curwensville's Oak Hill Cemetery.

V.   Fred J. (b. May 16, 1887; d. December 12, 1952) married Belle Reed Forcey (b. April 7, 1887; d. December 12, 1925) of Clearfield[vi]

VI.   Francis Ignatius, known to all as "Tucker," (b. May 10, 1891; d. January 1, 1962) married Roxie M. Hess (b. January 19, 1891; d. January 23, 1963), daughter of Abraham Hess of Clearfield[vii] (see more on William [Bill] Thompson)[viii]

VII.   A daughter who died in infancy (1892), possibly as a result of or causing the death of her mother in childbirth.[ix]

All four sons of Ignatius and Mary were said to be mechanically inclined. They established the original electric plant in Curwensville and assisted with the Clearfield plant, later branching out into new territory. They sold their interests to the Penn Public Corporation and established other businesses, including real estate, water companies, and theatres.

5th generation (dates align with the 7th generation of the John Pifer Paternal Lineage)

Howard Jefferson Thompson (b. January 12, 1878 in Curwensville; died January 3, 1968 in Clearfield) married **Elizabeth Bailey Spencer** (b. September 14, 1880 [An egregious error is the birth date on her tombstone of 1881; ALL records, including her obituary, use the correct date of 1880.][x] in Curwensville; d. October 10, 1951 in Clearfield), daughter of Vincent Uriah Spencer.

Howard Jefferson Thompson, known as H. J., was engaged in various successful businesses—water, electricity, coal, movie theatres, a knitting mill, and banking. He was president of the Cassidy Coal Company, Central Penn Light and Power Company, Curwensville Water Company, Curwensville State Bank, and Mid State Theatres, as well as co-owner of the knitting mill. Some would have called him the second Fred Dyer. He also ran twice for a seat in the Pennsylvania State Senate. Those who knew him would have described H. J. as "a hard man." Elizabeth shared in the ownership of the Mid State Theatres, retaining (protecting) her shares for her children.

Howard Jefferson Thompson and Elizabeth Bailey Spencer were married in a wedding (with R.K. Way standing as best man and Alice Bilger serving as her maid of honor) held in the bride's home on June 17, 1903.[xi] They are the parents of three children:

I.   **Howard Vincent** (b. April 10, 1904 in Clearfield; d. Jan. 14, 1964 in Clearfield) (8th)

      (see progeny below)

II.   Mary Alice (b. November 21, 1905 in Clearfield; d. April 19, 1998 in State College) first married William Kitson Jackson (b. December 28, 1906; d. February 23, 1945, a WWII casualty at Henri-Chapelle, Belgium). On December 28, 1946 Mary Alice married Bradford Blueford Crunk (b. February 16, 1914 in Lockhart, Texas; d. May 1, 1998 in State College). Mary Alice and William Jackson are the parents of one child:

William Spencer Jackson (b. September 4, 1934 in Philadelphia)[xii]; married Rosemary Keating in 1960. They are the parents of two children:

    I.   Tracy (Chloe Valeria and Kyleigh Rose)

    II. William Kitson II (Sage Marie and Kitson)

III. Philip Bell (b. October 20, 1919 in Bellefonte; d. January 21, 2001 in Altoona) married Eva Hart (b. June 15, 1922; d. September 4, 2010) circa 1951. They are the parents of two children:

    I.   Patricia Ann (b. April 25, 1952; d. December 17, 2008)

    II. Mark Allen (Jessica Sue Walters and Morgan Rae), Williamsburg, Virginia as of 2008

6th generation (dates align with the 8th generation of the John Pifer Paternal Lineage)

Howard Vincent Thompson, whose sister gave him the nickname "Bubby," was born in Clearfield, then moved to East Linn Street in Bellefonte after the age of six. The family later returned to Clearfield circa 1921. Bubby worked for his father most of his life, beginning in his early teens, reading meters, installing meters, and trimming street arcs. After attending Williamsport Business College, he served as secretary and treasurer of the Curwensville Water Company from 1925 until 1941 at which time he became manager of the Rex Theatre. In addition, he was a former Curwensville Borough tax collector, auditor, and minority inspector of the election board in Curwensville's First Ward. He later served as president of Mid State Theatres. He also was very active in Volunteer Firemen's Associations, the Loyal Order of Moose, and the IOOF.

Howard Vincent Thompson (b. April 10, 1904 in Clearfield; d. January 14, 1964 in Clearfield) married **Katherine Shields Pifer** (b. February 11, 1908 in Curwensville; d. January 31, 1998 in Hershey), daughter of John and Matilda Smith Pifer.

Howard Vincent Thompson and Catherine (as spelled on the marriage license) Shields Pifer were married on June 20, 1927. They are the parents of four daughters:

    I.   **Matilda Kay** (b. November 1, 1930 in Curwensville) (7th)

    II.   **Judith Evelyn** (b. March 9, 1937 in Clearfield) (7th)

    III. **Jo Ellen** (b. November 6, 1938 in Clearfield) (7th)

    IV. **Elizabeth Nan** (b. August 19, 1942 in Clearfield) (7th)

7th generation (dates align with the 9th generation of the John Pifer Paternal Lineage)

It was this generation who moved from Curwensville, each in turn after high school graduation: Kay moving to California, but returning to Curwensville in the late 1980s; Judith settling in Hummelstown, Pennsylvania to teach in the newly formed Lower Dauphin Junior-Senior High School; Jo Ellen leaving for government service and later working in her husband's CPA firm in the DC area; and Nan to DC, then California, returning to live in Hershey, Pennsylvania, where she worked in public relations and publications for the Penn State Medical Center, now as designer for Yesteryear Publishing.

At this point the genealogies merge and become one with the Thompson Sisters who originate through the marriage of Catherine Pifer and Howard V. Thompson.

As explained in the section on the Paternal Lineage of John Frederick Pifer, which was used as the baseline, the genealogies are aligned by the ages of those who lived at a common time. Because a lineage begins with the first generation of a family that could be found, a person identified in the third generation of one lineage might match in age to those in the sixth generation of another's lineage. For example, in this set of genealogies, persons named in the seventh generation of Elizabeth's Paternal Lineage, would match in age with those in the eighth generation of John Pifer's Maternal Lineage as well as in his Paternal Lineage because his ancestors on both sides (mother and father) are of the same timeframe (similar birth dates).

Most frequently a person appears in different generations in the separate lineages. For example, because Matilda Pifer's mother's lineage could not be traced back very many generations (There are no records for the key people), Catherine and Howard Thompson are only the third generation in her Maternal Lineage, but are **eighth** in John Pifer's Maternal Lineage—or even **27**[th] if we count the lineage back to William the Conqueror.

To demonstrate, those of the **1**[st] **generation** of Matilda Smith Pifer's **Maternal Lineage** would align with the following:

- **4th generation** of her own **Paternal Lineage**

- **4th generation** of H. J. Thompson's **Paternal Lineage**

- **5th generation** of Elizabeth Spencer Thompson's **Paternal Lineage**

- **6th generation** of Elizabeth's **Maternal Lineage** and of H. J.'s **Maternal Lineage**

- **6th generation** of John F. Pifer's **Maternal** and **Paternal Lineage** beginning in America or the 25th generation (if we include to William the Conqueror) of his **Maternal Lineage**

THE THOMPSON SISTERS ARE

9th generation of Howard Jefferson Thompson's Maternal Lineage
7th generation of his Paternal Lineage

9th generation of Elizabeth Spencer Thompson's Maternal Lineage
8th generation of her Paternal Lineage

9th (or 28th if we include back to William the Conqueror) generation of John Frederick Pifer's Maternal Lineage
9th generation of his Paternal Lineage

4th generation of Matilda Smith Pifer's Maternal Lineage
7th generation of her Paternal Lineage

Matilda Kay

Following graduation Kay, a talented dancer, went to Philadelphia and auditioned for a place in a music hall/theatre chorus line. After a year in Philadelphia and being wooed by the man "back home," she returned to Curwensville. However, the call of far-away places led her to leave her hometown for California where she worked for Pacific Mutual and about a year later found her dream job with Trans World Airlines.

On August 26, 1950 Matilda Kay Thompson married Albert R. Brunetti (born June 12, 1924; d. August 19, 2012; son of Oreste and Edith Durandetto Brunetti). They are the parents of one child, a daughter, Mavis Kim, born on September 2, 1952. Following a divorce from Albert Brunetti, years later on May 22, 1980 Kay married Robert A. Walker of Clearfield.

The child of Kay Thompson and Albert Brunetti

> Mavis Kim (b. September 2, 1952 in Clearfield) (8th)

8th generation (aligns with the 10th generation of the John Pifer Paternal Lineage [and the 5th generation of Matilda's Maternal Lineage])

Kim Richards lives in Cathedral City, California and is based in Palm Springs where she is a Buyer and Personal Shopper for Macy's. In 1970 Kim married Earl Richards, but the marriage later ended in divorce.

Judith Evelyn

Judith holds an earned doctorate in administration; served as a high school English teacher, teacher, principal, and assistant to the superintendent; worked for the Pennsylvania Department of Education; and is the Director of the Capital Area Institute for Mathematics and Science at Penn State Harrisburg. She also heads a private consulting business (Educon) and a publishing company (Yesteryear Publishing). In addition, she has chaired a number of major civic events and is the author of eighteen books, many on social history.

On September 6, 1958 Judith Evelyn Thompson (b. March 9, 1937) married Thomas Eugene Ball (b. January 31, 1937), son of Elmer and Rena Graham Ball. Following a divorce, on February 25, 1972 Judith married Walter C. Witmer (b. January 18, 1931; d. June 13, 2003), son of Miles and Ethel Espenshade Witmer).

The children of Judith Evelyn Thompson and Thomas Eugene Ball

> I.   Jean Rochelle (b. March 7, 1959 in Harrisburg) (8th)
>
> II.   Thomas Ross (b. April 23, 1968 in Camp Hill) (8th)

8th generation (aligns with the 10th generation of the John Pifer Paternal Lineage [and the 5th generation of Matilda's Maternal Lineage])

Jean Rochelle Ball Jacobs is the staff accountant for Kurtz Bros. in Clearfield, Pennsylvania. She married **James Gary Jacobs** (b. October 3, 1948) in 1984.

The children of Jean Rochelle Ball and James Jacobs

> I.   **Jordan Ashlee** (b. April 17, 1986 in Clearfield) (9th)
>
> II. **Jillian Rochelle** (b. October 29, 1992 in Clearfield) (9th)

Thomas Ross Ball is the owner of Thomas Ball Entertainment in Hershey, Pennsylvania. He married **Michelle Ann Garger** (b. 1971) in 2000; they were divorced in 2015.

The children of Thomas Ross Ball and Michelle Garger

> I.   **Emily Madison** (b. July 11, 2002 in Harrisburg) (9th)
>
> II. **Olivia Emerson** (b. June 27, 2005 in Harrisburg) (9th)

9th generation (aligns with the 11th generation of the John Pifer Paternal Lineage [and the 6th generation of Matilda's Maternal Lineage])

As of September 2015:

> **Jordan Ashlee Jacobs** is employed by Laborers Int'l. Union of North America 158 HCL.
>
> **Jillian Rochelle Jacobs** is Hospital Operations Coordinator for United Health Services.
>
> **Emily Madison Ball** is in eighth grade at the Lower Dauphin Middle School.
>
> **Olivia Emerson Ball** is in fifth grade at Conewago Elementary School.

Jo Ellen

Jo Ellen began her professional career with the Federal Bureau of Investigation (FBI) in Washington, DC, followed by a position with the National Security Agency (the top intelligence organization of the U.S. government), then the newest government agency—later to become the premium agency with the highest clearances required—where she quickly earned a high-level administrative position. She later joined her husband in his business, Lorenz and Lorenz Certified Public Accountants.

On September 6, 1958, in a double wedding ceremony shared with her sister Judith, **Jo Ellen Thompson** (b. November 6, 1938) married **Eugene Kendall Lorenz** (b. September 19, 1932), the son of Alma ("Bonnie") Corinne Miller and Eugene Hurdle Lorenz.

The children of Jo Ellen Thompson and Eugene Kendall Lorenz

> I.   **Janelle Corinne Lorenz Wright** (b. January 2, 1969) (8th)
>
> II. **Eugene Kendall Lorenz, Jr.** (b. April 17, 1970; d. January 3, 2013) (8th)

8ᵗʰ generation (aligns with the 10ᵗʰ generation of the John Pifer Paternal Lineage [and the 5ᵗʰ generation of Matilda's Maternal Lineage])

Janelle Lorenz Wright manages real estate for her parents and her family. Previously, she was employed by KPMG Peat Marwick and as the private label buyer for Saks Fifth Avenue's catalog division.

Janelle Lorenz married **Jay Oscar Wright** (b. December 12, 1969, St. Johnsbury, Vermont) on October 25, 1997. They reside in Potomac, Maryland. They are the parents of

    I. **Corinne Catherine Wright** (b. May 29, 2001 in Sarasota, Florida) (9ᵗʰ)

    II. **Theodore Piers Wright** (b. September 30, 2002 in Silver Spring, Maryland) (9ᵗʰ)

9ᵗʰ generation (aligns with the 11ᵗʰ generation of the John Pifer Paternal Lineage [and the 6ᵗʰ generation of Matilda's Maternal Lineage])

As of September 2015:

    Corinne Catherine Wright is in the ninth grade at The Connelly School of the Holy Child, Potomac, Maryland.

    Theodore Piers Wright is in the sixth grade at Echelon Academy, Sandy Spring, Maryland.

Elizabeth Nan

Nan began her professional career with the National Security Agency in Washington, DC. She later moved to Southern California where she worked for the City of Anaheim. Following a return to Pennsylvania, she worked in Development for Dickinson College in Carlisle before finding her niche in Public Relations for Penn State's College of Medicine and Hershey Medical Center. Currently she manages and is the page designer for Yesteryear Publishing.

On August 18, 1965 **Elizabeth Nan Thompson** (b. August 19, 1942) married **Joel Keith Edmunds** (b. August 14, 1942), the son of Irvin C. and Jaclyn Beck Edmunds.

The children of Elizabeth Nan Thompson and Joel Keith Edmunds

    I. **Shayne Scott Edmunds** (b. December 9, 1965 in Northridge, California) (8ᵗʰ)

    II. **Jesse Joel Edmunds** (b. November 6, 1979 in Lucerne Valley, California) (8ᵗʰ)

8ᵗʰ generation (aligns with the 10ᵗʰ generation of the John Pifer Paternal Lineage [and the 5ᵗʰ generation of Matilda's Maternal Lineage])

Shayne Edmunds and his wife, **Grace Graybill,** are co-owners of the Neato Burrito restaurant chain located throughout South Central Pennsylvania.

Shayne Edmunds married **Ada Grace Graybill** (b. November 10, 1969) on June 15, 1999. They reside in Dillsburg, Pennsylvania and are the parents of

    I.   **Aero Graham** (b. April 18, 2004 in Harrisburg, Pennsylvania) (9th)

    II. **Iris Isadora** (b. September 2, 2005 in Harrisburg, Pennsylvania) (9th)

Jesse Edmunds is an outdoor adventurer as well as an accomplished musician who currently performs in the Greater Harrisburg, Pennsylvania area. He resides in Hershey, Pennsylvania.

9th generation (aligns with the 11th generation of the John Pifer Paternal Lineage [and the 6th generation of Matilda's Maternal Lineage])

As of September 2015:

    Aero Graham is in the sixth grade at Northern Middle School in Dillsburg, Pennsylvania.

    Iris Isadora is in the fifth grade at Northern Elementary School in Dillsburg, Pennsylvania.

---

i   The number of children is noted here only because some of the early historical resources used these numbers only with the names of the women.

ii   Henrietta married Frederick Johnson (Fred J.) Dyer (information included here because of interest in the Dyer building in Curwensville). Frederick Dyer (1858-1926) was not born in Curwensville but moved there and was engaged in various businesses, operating a sawmill, match factory, tanning company, and holding mercantile interests (hence the store aforementioned). He was instrumental in securing the PA Hide and Leather Company to locate in Curwensville and "was for a number of years considered Curwensville's foremost businessman." The Dyers were the aunt and uncle of H. J. Thompson. Their youngest daughter Miriam (b. 1897; d. 1963) was the wife of Karl Hamilton (1893-1979), likely the brother of Droz who married Josephine Pifer. (Shaw's Genealogies). Miriam and Karl had a daughter Henrietta Hamilton (1925-1957).

iii Ancestry.com has the wrong death date of 1919.

iv New information to me as of September 2015, with the only record being a tombstone; however, the Fleming Family Tree identifies baby Erie as female.

v   The details are included here as Walter left Curwensville and never returned. We Thompson sisters did not know there was a great-uncle Walter or that our father had a cousin Irene.

vi Fred's children were Frederick, Mary Elizabeth, Jane, and Maud Ann.

vii Francis' children were Darl Francis, Robert Walter, Lois May, and William Lee.

viii William, the youngest of this generation of Thompson siblings and cousins, was a well-known designer of period rooms, particularly those in New York City mansions and Southern plantations owned by Richard Jenrette, Bill's life partner and a well-known financier, who collected and restored antebellum residences. Bill's work was featured at the Antiques Show in the NYC Armory in the 1990s (which Judith attended). He and Jenrette divided their time among Charleston, SC, a New York City brownstone, Edgewater, once owned by Gore Vidal, in Watertown, NY, and other properties. Bill has authored *Beginnings* and *Ghostly Poems*. Richard Jenrette's book *Adventures with Old Houses* includes a foreword by the Prince of Wales.

ix There is a possibility that this child's birth and death date is wrong here and that the death in infancy is Baby Erie born/died in 1872. I have not been able to confirm this.

x   An insulting and careless error (not corrected) that upset her son Howard, adding to the already severed relationship between father and son.

xi An account of the wedding appeared in the local paper, calling this event "a wedding of some note."

xii In 1948 Bill Jackson was legally adopted by Bradford B. Crunk, but retained (at Mr. Crunk's insistence) the name of his birth father "to always honor him," as Brad noted.

Maternal Lineage

for

Howard Jefferson Thompson

Maternal Lineage for Howard Jefferson Thompson

Part I

"The Bells" – Mary Erie Bell's Maternal Lineage

In 1738 the good ship *Glasgow* first set sail from Rotterdam, Europe's largest port, and then left from the port in Cowes, on the northern point of the Isle of Wight, England, headed for America (An immigration date is given as June 22, 1738 which may be the date of departure). The *Glasgow* entered the Philadelphia harbor on September 9. One of the passengers was **John Frederick Zinn** (Johannes Zinn on the manifest) (b. 1706 in Plohnheim, Baden-Wuerttemberg, Germany) who had married **Anna Sophia Schneider** (b. August 1, 1706 in Plohnheim; d. September 21, 1770 in Dover, Pennsylvania). Frederick and Anna were married at Mederon in die Pfalz, Germany in 1726, twelve years before leaving Germany to come to America. (The passenger list has the names of only the male passengers; however, there are three with the surname of Schneider so perhaps other family members of Anna sailed as well.)

1st generation (dates align with generations as numbered in the John Pifer Paternal Lineage)

After arriving in Philadelphia, **Johannes (John) Frederick Zinn** and **Anna Sophia Schneider Zinn** settled in Lancaster, Pennsylvania and lived there for a short time. John Frederick then purchased approximately two hundred acres of land from William Penn, territory Penn had been granted by the King of England against debts owed to Penn's father.

Anna was 31 years of age at this point. Their first child (Philip Jacob Zinn) had been born to them in Kederon, Germany and was one year of age when his parents sailed for America.

   I.   **Philip Jacob Zinn** (b. May 25, 1737; d. May 4, 1809) (2nd)

The following are the other identified children of John Zinn and Anna Schneider who were born in America:

   II.   Johan (John) Nicholas Zinn (b. November, 1739; d. 1823)

   III.   Maria Margaret (b. 1740)

   IV.   Anna Catherine Zinn (b. January 18 [or May 20], 1745; d. 1811)

2nd generation (dates align with generations as numbered in the John Pifer Paternal Lineage)

Philip Jacob Zinn grew to manhood on his father's farm, which he then purchased from his father in 1763. Philip was married twice, being widowed when his first wife died at a young age.

1st marriage.

Philip Jacob Zinn married **Marie Elizabeth Bartmess** (b. March 3, 1738 in Wahlenau, Rhineland-Palatinate, Germany; d. October 10, 1771) who had come to America with her brother Peter. The parents of Marie Elizabeth were Johannes Petrus Bartmess and Ana Maria Frantz.

Philip and Marie Elizabeth were married in 1757 and are the parents of the following children:

I.   Margaret (b. 1756; d. 1809) married John Kramer

II.   James Frederick (b. 1758; d. 1809)

III.   Johannes (b. October 30, 1761; d. 1817) married Mary E. Beitzel

IV.   Maria [or Anna] Elizabeth (b. December 9, 1762; d. 1845)

V.   Margaret (All Ancestry.com records show two children named Margaret, the second born in 1765. However, since the number 65 is a transposition of 56, this could be a clerical error. I could find no further information.)

VI.   John Philip (b. August 3, 1766; d. 1871)

VII.   John Adam (b. August 30, 1768; d. 1771)

VIII. John Jacob (b. August 22, 1769; d. circa 1841) married Catherine Raffensberger

IX.   **Catherine** (b. 1770 in York; d. October 24, 1843 in Clearfield) (3rd)

2nd marriage.

On April 5, 1772 in Dover, Pennsylvania Philip Jacob Zinn married Anna Kinta Hoffman (b. 1741 in Lancaster, Pennsylvania; d. May 16, 1784).

The children of Philip Zinn and Anna Kinta Cunigunda Hoffman (If the dates of birth are correct, these children were all born when their mother was in her thirties.)[i]

I.   Nicholas (b. July 30, 1773; d. 1852) married Magdalena Shaffer in 1795

II.   Anna Maria (b. October 15, 1774; d. 1815)

III.   Mary (b. 1775)

IV.   Barbara (b. June 2, 1776)

V.   Magdalena (b. June 21, 1778; d. 1834)

VI.   Christiana (b. 1779; d. 1808)

3rd generation (dates align with generations as numbered in the John Pifer Paternal Lineage)

Catherine Zinn (b. 1770; d. October 24, 1843) married **Martin Johann Hoover** (b. September 5, 1762 in York, Pennsylvania; d. June 6, 1841 in Clearfield County), the son of Johannes Conrad and Anna Maria Lentz Hoover. Martin's father, Conrad Hoover, had been born in Laubia, Germany in 1734 and had come to America on August 25, 1761, settling in York County, Pennsylvania.

The date of 1788 is given as the marriage of Catherine Zinn and Martin Hoover and they are said to have been the parents of seven children. However, one source had listed names of twelve progeny; another source indicated that they were the parents of 15 children. One list omitted Mary "Polly" but included all other names, beginning with Daniel and ending with Esther. All are included in the following list, as I found evidence of the missing five in an additional source. There is also a listing of a first child, with the birth date given as before the marriage of Catherine and Martin (Of course, it is always possible that dates or records are in error):

I.   Martin Hoover (b. 1784)

II.   John (b. 1788/89; d. 1841) married Mollie G. Reynolds

III.   Samuel (b. December 14, 1790; d. 1835)

IV.   Jacob (b. March 16, 1792; d. 1881)

V.   Elizabeth (b. September 14, 1793; d. 1882)

VI.   Mary Polly (b. April 12, 1794; d. 1825)

VII.   **Joseph Martin** (b. March 1, 1795; d. November 29, 1879) (4th)

VIII. Daniel (b. 1797; d. 1841) OR (b. 1794; d. 1847)

IX.   George (b. 1799; d. 1824)

X.   David (b. October 5, 1801; d. May 7, 1853)

XI.   Nancy Ann (b. August 25, 1802 in Lawrence Township; d. September 6, 1879; married Rev. John Flegal)

XII.   Catherine (b. 1806 in Reynoldsville; d. 1834) OR (b. 1781; d.1834)

XIII. Esther Hetty (b. 1810/08; d. 1843) OR (b. 1782)

4th generation (dates align with generations as numbered in the John Pifer Paternal Lineage)

Joseph Martin Hoover (b. March 1, 1795 in Centre County; d. 1879 in Pike Township) married Rebecca Price (b. 1798; d. 1879).

Joseph M. Hoover and Rebecca Price were married on October 08/28, 1817 and are the parents of the following children:

I.   Mary Ann (b. July 5, 1818; d. July 8, 1904)

II.   Libbeus Luther (b. October 19, 1819; d. April 30, 1889)

III.   Elizabeth (b. June 15, 1821; d. September 12, 1904)

IV.   Martha (b. Feb. 3, 1823; d. September 15, 1853)

V.   Cynthia (b. November 2, 1824; d. May 26, 1904)

VI.   **Margery** (b. July 30, 1826; d. December 22, 1860/69) (5th)

VII.   Hannah M. (b. February 22, 1828; d. November 16, 1863)

VIII. Thomas Alexander (b. April 28, 1830; d. October 18, 1882)

IX.   Clarinda (b. December 6, 1832; d. January 10, 1897)

X.   Ross McClure (b. October 25, 1833; d. February 24, 1892)

XI.   Rachel Jane (b. March 8, 1835)

XII.   William Caldwell (b. March 12, 1838; d. September 6, 1918)

XIII.   Catherine (b. January 13, 1840; d. June 11, 1919)

5th generation (dates align with generations as numbered in the John Pifer Paternal Lineage)

Margery Hoover (b. July 30, 1826; d. December 22, 1860[ii]) married David R. Bell (b. February 11, 1824; d. December 31, 1875), son of Greenwood and Elizabeth Roll Bell. All were of Greenwood Township in Clearfield County.

Margery Hoover and David R. Bell were married in 1844 and are the parents of the following children:

I.   **Mary Erie** (b. August 15, 1850; d. March 10, 1892) (6th)

II.   Martha J. (b. May 6, 1852; d. February 11, 1864)

III.   Winfield Scott (b. November 11, 1853; d. June 17, 1898) married Minerva Arthurs

IV.   Jefferson (b. 1854)

6th generation (dates align with generations as numbered in the John Pifer Paternal Lineage)

Mary Erie Bell (b. August 15, 1850; d. March 10, 1892) married **Francis Ignatius Thompson** (b. June 2, 1846; d. 1909).

Mary Erie Bell and Francis Ignatius Thompson are the parents of the following:

I.   Erie (b. January 28, 1872; d. February 19, 1872[iii])

II.   Walter B. (possibly Bell; b. January 1874; d. February 14, 1946) He first married Edna M. Thompson (this may or may not be her maiden name) (b. March 1881) in 1900. He later married Charlotte Decker (b. 1890; d. October 1968), daughter of Mary Henderson and David Bell (some sources suggest Charlotte's name was Charlotte Decker Bell). Walter and Charlotte were married on December 28, 1910 when he was 36 and she was 20 and they are the parents of one daughter, Irene, born in 1912. Walter and Charlotte are interred in the Greenlawn Cemetery in Salem, Massachusetts.[iv]

III.   **Howard Jefferson** (b. January 12, 1878; d. January 3, 1968), whose middle name was chosen to honor the name of his mother's brother. (7th)

IV.   Maud A. (b. June 10, 1884; d. September 30, 1958) married Clinton Davidson (b. 1882); was widowed, then lived with a Mr. Stamp in Buffalo, NY. (We were told Aunt Maud kept house for Mr. Stamp.) Her family honored her wishes to be interred in the family's section in Curwensville's Oak Hill Cemetery.

V.   Fred J. (b. May 16, 1887; d. December 12, 1952) married Belle Reed Forcey (b. April 7, 1887; d. December 12, 1925) of Clearfield[v]

VI. Francis Ignatius, known to all as "Tucker," (b. May 10, 1891; d. January 1, 1962) married Roxie M. Hess (b. January 19, 1891; d. January 23, 1963), daughter of Abraham Hess of Clearfield[vi] (see more on William [Bill] Thompson) [vii]

VII. A daughter who died in infancy (1892), possibly as a result, or causing the death, of her mother in childbirth.[viii]

7th generation (dates align with generations as numbered in the John Pifer Paternal Lineage)

All four sons of Ignatius and Mary were said to be mechanically inclined. They established the original electric plant in Curwensville and assisted with the Clearfield electric plant, later branching out into new territory. They sold their interests to the Penn Public Corporation and established other businesses, including real estate, water companies, and theatres.

Howard Jefferson Thompson (b. January 12, 1878 in Curwensville; d. January 3, 1968 in Clearfield) married Elizabeth Bailey Spencer (b. September 14, 1880[ix] in Curwensville; d. October 10, 1951 in Clearfield), daughter of Vincent Uriah Spencer.

Howard Jefferson Thompson, known as H. J., was engaged in various successful businesses—water, electricity, coal, movie theatres, a knitting mill, and banking. He was president of the Cassidy Coal Company, Central Penn Light and Power Company, Curwensville Water Company, Curwensville State Bank, and Mid State Theatres, as well as co-owner of the knitting mill. Some would have called him the second Fred Dyer. He also ran twice for a seat in the Pennsylvania State Senate. Those who knew him would have described H. J. as "a hard man." Elizabeth shared in the ownership of the Mid State Theatres, retaining (protecting) her shares for her children.

Howard Jefferson Thompson and Elizabeth Bailey Spencer Thompson were married in a wedding of some note held at the home of the bride on the morning of June 17, 1903. They are the parents of the following children:

I.   Howard Vincent (b. April 10, 1904 in Clearfield; d. Jan. 14, 1964 in Clearfield) (8th) (see progeny below)

II. Mary Alice (b. November 21, 1905 in Clearfield; d. April 19, 1998 in State College) first married William Kitson Jackson (b. December 28, 1906; d. February 23, 1945, a WWII casualty at Henri-Chapelle, Belgium). On December 28, 1946 Mary Alice married Bradford Blueford Crunk (b. February 16, 1914 in Lockhart, Texas; d. May 1, 1998 in State College). Mary Alice and William Jackson are the parents of one child:

William Spencer Jackson (b. September 4, 1934 in Philadelphia)[x]; married Rosemary Keating in 1960. They are the parents of two children:

I.   Tracy (Chloe Valeria and Kyleigh Rose)

II. William Kitson II (Sage Marie and Kitson)

III. Philip Bell (b. October 20, 1919 in Bellefonte; d. January 21, 2001 in Altoona) married Eva Hart (b. June 15, 1922; d. September 4, 2010) circa 1951. They are the parents of two children:

  I.   Patricia Ann (b. April 25, 1952; d. December 17, 2008)
  II. Mark Allen (Jessica Sue Walters and Morgan Rae), Williamsburg, Virginia as of 2008

8th generation (dates align with generations as numbered in the John Pifer Paternal Lineage)

Howard Vincent Thompson, whose sister gave him the nickname "Bubby," was born in Clearfield, then moved to East Linn Street in Bellefonte after the age of six. The family later returned to Clearfield circa 1921. Bubby worked for his father most of his life, beginning in his early teens, reading meters, installing meters, and trimming street arcs. After attending Williamsport Business College, he served as secretary and treasurer of the Curwensville Water Company from 1925 until 1941 at which time he became manager of the Rex Theatre. In addition, he was a former Curwensville Borough tax collector, auditor, and minority inspector of the election board in Curwensville's First Ward. He later served as president of Mid State Theatres. He also was very active in Volunteer Firemen's Associations, the Loyal Order of Moose, and the IOOF.

Howard Vincent Thompson (b. April 10, 1904 in Clearfield; d. January 14, 1964 in Clearfield) married **Katherine Shields Pifer** (b. February 11, 1908 in Curwensville; d. January 31, 1998 in Hershey), daughter of John and Matilda Smith Pifer.

Howard Vincent Thompson and Katherine Shields Pifer were married on June 20, 1927 (officiated by the Reverend Edward C. Reeve) and are the parents of the following four daughters:

  I.   **Matilda Kay** (b. November 1, 1930 in Curwensville) (9th)
  II.   **Judith Evelyn** (b. March 9, 1937 in Clearfield) (9th)
  III. **Jo Ellen** (b. November 6, 1938 in Clearfield) (9th)
  IV.   **Elizabeth Nan** (b. August 19, 1942 in Clearfield) (9th)

9th generation (dates align with generations as numbered in the John Pifer Paternal Lineage)

It was this generation who moved from Curwensville, each in turn, after high school graduation: Kay moving to California, but returning to Curwensville in the late 1980s; Judith settling in Hummelstown, Pennsylvania to teach in the newly formed Lower Dauphin Junior-Senior High School; Jo Ellen leaving for government service and later working in her husband's CPA firm in the DC area; and Nan to DC, then California, returning to live in Hershey, Pennsylvania, where she worked in public relations and publications for the Penn State Medical Center, now as designer for Yesteryear Publishing.

At this point the genealogies merge and become one with the Thompson Sisters who originate through the marriage of Catherine Pifer and Howard V. Thompson.

As explained in the section on the Paternal Lineage of John Frederick Pifer, which was used as the baseline, the genealogies are aligned by the ages of those who lived at a common time. Because a lineage begins with the first generation of a family that could be found, a person identified in the third generation of one lineage might match in age to those in the sixth generation of another's lineage. For example, in this set of genealogies, persons named in the seventh generation of Elizabeth's Paternal Lineage, would match in age with those in the eighth generation of John Pifer's Maternal Lineage as well as in his Paternal Lineage because his ancestors on both sides (mother and father) are of the same timeframe (similar birth dates).

Most frequently a person appears in different generations in the separate lineages. For example, because Matilda Pifer's mother's lineage could not be traced back very many generations (There are no records for the key people), Catherine and Howard Thompson are only the third generation in her Maternal Lineage, but are **eighth** in John Pifer's Maternal Lineage—or even **27**[th] if we count the lineage back to William the Conqueror.

To demonstrate, those of the **1**[st] **generation** of Matilda Smith Pifer's **Maternal Lineage** would align with the following:

- **4th generation** of her own **Paternal Lineage**
- **4th generation** of H. J. Thompson's **Paternal Lineage**
- **5th generation** of Elizabeth Spencer Thompson's **Paternal Lineage**
- **6th generation** of Elizabeth's **Maternal Lineage** and of H. J.'s **Maternal Lineage**
- **6th generation** of John F. Pifer's **Maternal Lineage** and **Paternal Lineage** beginning in America or the 25th generation (if we include to William the Conqueror) of his **Maternal Lineage**

THE THOMPSON SISTERS ARE

9th generation of Howard Jefferson Thompson's Maternal Lineage
7th generation of his Paternal Lineage

9th generation of Elizabeth Spencer Thompson's Maternal Lineage
8th generation of her Paternal Lineage

9th (or 28th if we include back to William the Conqueror) generation of John Frederick Pifer's Maternal Lineage
9th generation of his Paternal Lineage

4th generation of Matilda Smith Pifer's Maternal Lineage
7th generation of her Paternal Lineage

Matilda Kay

Following graduation Kay, a talented dancer, went to Philadelphia and auditioned for a place in a music hall/theatre chorus line. After a year in Philadelphia and being wooed by the man "back home," she returned to Curwensville. However, the call of far-away places led her to leave her hometown for California where she worked for Pacific Mutual and about a year later found her dream job with Trans World Airlines.

On August 26, 1950 **Matilda Kay Thompson** married **Albert R. Brunetti** (born June 12, 1924; d. August 19, 2012; son of Oreste and Edith Durandetto Brunetti). They are the parents of one child, a daughter, Mavis Kim, born on September 2, 1952. Following a divorce from Albert Brunetti, years later on May 22, 1980 Kay married **Robert A. Walker** of Clearfield.

The child of Kay Thompson and Albert Brunetti

> **Mavis Kim** (b. September 2, 1952 in Clearfield) **(10th)**

10th generation (dates align with the 10th generation of the John Pifer Paternal Lineage)

Kim Richards lives in Cathedral City, California and is based in Palm Springs where she is a Buyer and Personal Shopper for Macy's. In 1970 Kim married Earl Richards, but the marriage later ended in divorce.

Judith Evelyn

Judith holds an earned doctorate in administration; served as a high school English teacher, principal, and assistant to the superintendent; worked for the Pennsylvania Department of Education; and is the Director of the Capital Area Institute for Mathematics and Science at Penn State Harrisburg. She also heads a private consulting business (Educon) and a publishing company (Yesteryear Publishing). In addition, she has chaired a number of major civic events and is the author of eighteen books, many on social history.

On September 6, 1958 **Judith Evelyn Thompson** (b. March 9, 1937) married **Thomas Eugene Ball** (b. January 31, 1937), son of Elmer and Rena Graham Ball. Following a divorce, on February 25, 1972 Judith married **Walter C. Witmer** (b. January 18, 1931; d. June 13, 2003), son of Miles and Ethel Espenshade Witmer).

The children of Judith Thompson and Thomas Ball

> I. Jean Rochelle Ball (b. March 7, 1959 in Harrisburg) **(10th)**
> II. Thomas Ross Ball (b. April 23, 1968 in Camp Hill) **(10th)**

10th generation (dates align with the 10th generation of the John Pifer Paternal Lineage)

Jean Rochelle Ball Jacobs is the staff accountant for Kurtz Bros. in Clearfield, Pennsylvania. She married James Gary Jacobs (b. October 3, 1948) in 1984.

The children of Jean Rochelle Ball and James Jacobs

    I.   **Jordan Ashlee** (b. April 17, 1986 in Clearfield) (11th)

    II.   **Jillian Rochelle** (b. October 29, 1992 in Clearfield) (11th)

Thomas Ross Ball is the owner of Thomas Ball Entertainment in Hershey, Pennsylvania. He married **Michelle Ann Garger** (b. 1971) in 2000; they were divorced in 2015. The children of Thomas Ross Ball and Michelle Garger

    I.   **Emily Madison** (b. July 11, 2002 in Harrisburg) (11th)

    II.   **Olivia Emerson** (b. June 27, 2005 in Harrisburg) (11th)

11th generation (dates align with the 11th generation of the John Pifer Paternal Lineage)

As of September 2015:

    Jordan Ashlee Jacobs is employed by Laborers Int'l. Union of North America 158 HCL.

    Jillian Rochelle Jacobs is Hospital Operations Coordinator for United Health Services.

    Emily Madison Ball is in eighth grade at the Lower Dauphin Middle School.

    Olivia Emerson Ball is in fifth grade at Conewago Elementary School.

Jo Ellen

Jo Ellen began her professional career with the Federal Bureau of Investigation (FBI) in Washington, DC, followed by a position with the National Security Agency (the top intelligence organization of the U.S. government), then the newest government agency—later to become the premium agency with the highest clearances required—where she quickly earned a high-level administrative position. She later joined her husband in his business, Lorenz and Lorenz Certified Public Accountants.

On September 6, 1958, **Jo Ellen Thompson** (b. November 6, 1938) married **Eugene Kendall Lorenz** (b. September 19, 1932), the son of Alma ("Bonnie") Corinne Miller and Eugene Hurdle Lorenz.

The children of Jo Ellen Thompson and Eugene Kendall Lorenz

    I. **Janelle Corinne Lorenz Wright** (b. January 2, 1969) (10th)

    II. **Eugene Kendall Lorenz, Jr.** (b. April 17, 1970; d. January 3, 2013) (10th)

10th generation (dates align with the 10th generation of the John Pifer Paternal Lineage)

Janelle Lorenz Wright manages real estate for her parents and family. Previously, she was employed by KPMG Peat Marwick and as the private label buyer for Saks Fifth Avenue's catalog division.

Janelle Lorenz married **Jay Oscar Wright** (b. December 12, 1969, St. Johnsbury, Vermont) on October 25, 1997. They reside in Potomac, Maryland. They are the parents of

    I. **Corinne Catherine Wright** (b. May 29, 2001 in Sarasota, Florida) (11th)

    II. **Theodore Piers Wright** (b. September 30, 2002 in Silver Spring, Maryland) (11th)

11th generation (dates align with the 11th generation of the John Pifer Paternal Lineage)

As of September 2015:

> Corinne Catherine Wright is in the ninth grade at The Connelly School of the Holy Child, Potomac, Maryland.

> Theodore Piers Wright is in the sixth grade at Echelon Academy, Sandy Spring, Maryland.

Elizabeth Nan

Nan began her professional career with the National Security Agency in Washington, DC. She later moved to Southern California where she worked for the City of Anaheim. Following a return to Pennsylvania, she worked in Development for Dickinson College in Carlisle before finding her niche in Public Relations for Penn State's College of Medicine and Hershey Medical Center. Currently she manages and is the page designer for Yesteryear Publishing.

On August 18, 1965 Elizabeth Nan Thompson (b. August 19, 1942) married Joel Keith Edmunds (b. August 14, 1942), the son of Irvin C. and Jaclyn Beck Edmunds.

The children of Elizabeth Nan Thompson and Joel Keith Edmunds

> I.   Shayne Scott Edmunds (b. December 9, 1965 in Northridge, California) (10th)

> II. Jesse Joel Edmunds (b. November 6, 1979 in Lucerne Valley, California) (10th)

10th generation (dates align with the 10th generation of the John Pifer Paternal Lineage)

Shayne Edmunds and his wife, Grace Graybill, are co-owners of the Neato Burrito restaurant chain located throughout South Central Pennsylvania.

Shayne Edmunds married Ada Grace Graybill (b. November 10, 1969) on June 15, 1999. They reside in Dillsburg, Pennsylvania and are the parents of

> I.   Aero Graham (b. April 18, 2004 in Harrisburg, Pennsylvania) (11th)

> II. Iris Isadora (b. September 2, 2005 in Harrisburg, Pennsylvania) (11th)

Jesse Edmunds is an outdoor adventurer as well as an accomplished musician who currently performs in the Greater Harrisburg, Pennsylvania area. He resides in Hershey, Pennsylvania.

11th generation (dates align with the 11th generation of the John Pifer Paternal Lineage)

As of September 2015:

> Aero Graham is in the sixth grade at Northern Middle School in Dillsburg, Pennsylvania.

> Iris Isadora is in the fifth grade at Northern Elementary School in Dillsburg, Pennsylvania.

i   Note the large number of years between the birth dates of (16) Laurence and (17) Laurence, all the more reason to assume there is an unidentified generation here.

ii   www.avocadoridge.com/carney/getperson.php?personID=12836&tree=tree1&tngprint...

iii   "Frontier Forts of Pennsylvania," V. II, pp. 241, 244, 284.

iv   Vol. 5, pp. 653-654.

v   From *The Story of Kate and Howard*: Nearby Brockwayville was home to various newspapers, one of which was *The Dubois Evening Express,* started in 1883, becoming a daily in 1893; Richard (Dick) Pifer, brother of John Pifer, served a time as editor Another of several newspapers in this small city was *The Morning Herald*, published by Charles J. Bangert and V. King Pifer, a cousin to John Pifer.

vi   There are inconsistencies throughout with the birth date of John F. Pifer; the memory card at his memorial service gave the birth date as 1886, which is obviously a misprint and was intended to be 1868; Ancestry.com uses 1867.

vii   It was this gentleman's daughter or perhaps daughter-in-law who sent a note to my mother (who would have been a cousin to Catherine Princetta) of Catherine Princetta's passing. At the time my mother wondered who this Mrs. Bowser was. As I recall, there was no return address, just a postmark on the envelope.

viii   This dress is framed and still in the possession of the family.

iv   Mother told us that this is the spelling Howard used and she continued with it.

x   Howard used the "Jr." designation even though his middle name was not that of his father.

Part II

"The Bells" – Mary Erie Bell's Paternal Lineage

Tracing the history from Mary Erie Bell's paternal side of the family

It had been bothering me that until recently I had not been able to locate information about Mary Erie Bell, the mother of Howard Jefferson Thompson and the great-grandmother of the Thompson sisters, Kay, Judith, Jo Ellen, and Nan. I wanted to know more about Mary Bell and was determined to conduct one last search which, this time, brought a new line to trace. As can happen with a misspelling of a name or a wrong date of birth in the database, I kept coming to dead ends until finally today (9/2/15) on Ancestry.com, I made a breakthrough.

This information will serve as an addition to the full Maternal Lineage for Howard Jefferson Thompson, "The Bells," as it traces the lineage of Mary Erie's mother and follows it through to the marriage of David R. Bell (This in itself had been an impediment, as my information listed his name as David P. Bell, and, to confuse things even further, in the same family **with the same parents** were a "David Bell" and later a "David R. Bell" (listed.)

Thus we begin this genealogy line with the marriage of **Johnannes Lawrenson Opdike** (b. 1651; d. 1729) and **Catherine Tryntye** (b. 1653; d. 1728). The parents of Johnannes and those of Catherine are to this point unknown. The birth dates of this couple (Johannes and Catherine) precede the dates marking the system I had established with the Paternal Lineage for John Pifer, which became the template for all eight sets of lineage. Because these first maternal ancestors of Howard J. Thompson were in America prior to the arbitrary early 18th Century cornerstone date I had designated as being **1st generation,** we will designate this couple (Johnannes and Catherine) as **1st generation minus one** or **pre-1st generation**, in order to keep the already established system intact.

Johannes Lawrenson Opdike was born in 1651 in Dutch Kills, Long Island, and Catherine Tryntye was born in 1653 in Long Island City, New York. It is likely, but not confirmed, that they were both of Dutch heritage.

Johannes and Catherine were married in 1669 in Queens, New York. This marriage produced but one child, Agnes, whose last name is spelled Opdyck, using the un-Anglicized spelling and adding more credence to the supposition of an ancestry in The Netherlands. Agnes was born in 1690 in Hunterdon County, New Jersey when Catherine was age 37. The reason for her parents' move from New York State is not known.

Agnes Opdyck, deemed 1ˢᵗ generation for purposes of this writing, married William Critchfield (b. 1686; d. May 6, 1773) in 1717 when she was 27 years of age. Both of her parents lived to witness this marriage and to enjoy the birth of their daughter's child in 1727 in Lebanon, New Jersey, when Agnes was the same age as her mother Catherine had been when Agnes was born. The child, **Elizabeth**, was only a year old when Agnes' mother Catherine passed away in Hopewell, Hunterdon, New Jersey. A year later, Agnes' father died and in 1739 Agnes died at age 49 when her daughter was only twelve. Agnes is part of the generation that is being designated in this Genealogy of the Thompson Sisters as the 1ˢᵗ generation (when aligned to the John Pifer template).

Elizabeth Critchfield (b. 1727; d. 1786) (2ⁿᵈ generation), daughter of William and Agnes, married John Frampton (b. 1714; d. 1784) in 1740 in Burlington, New Jersey when Elizabeth was only thirteen years of age. Elizabeth and John also were the parents of only one child in their marriage. This child, a daughter named Mary, was born in 1758 in Trenton, New Jersey when Elizabeth was 31 years old. Both Elizabeth and John died in Mifflin County, Pennsylvania.

Mary Frampton (b. 1758; d. July 6, 1829) (3ʳᵈ generation), daughter of Elizabeth and John, married John Roll (b. January 12, 1755; d. January 15, 1816) on July 14, 1781 in Cumberland County, Pennsylvania when she was 23 years of age and while both of her parents were still living. (The John Roll that Mary Frampton married was the son of Mary Nevis and John Roll.)

Mary Frampton Roll gave birth to a daughter as well, and named the child (I.) Mary (b. October 6, 1783; d. 1862). This child was born in Clarion, Pennsylvania. Mary and John then had three additional daughters born to them:

    II.   Joanna (b. June 16, 1786 in Centre County; d. 1843)

    III.   Elizabeth (4ᵗʰ generation) (b. November 14, 1787 in Clearfield, Pennsylvania; d. 1850)

    IV.   Hetty (b. December 23, 1799 in Clearfield; d. 1868)

Both Mary and John Roll died in Clarion County, she at age 71 and he at age 61.

Elizabeth Roll (4ᵗʰ generation) (b. November 14, 1787; d. May 15, 1850 in Clearfield) married Greenwood Bell (b. November 20, 1785; d. September 8, 1860) on December 26, 1809 in Clearfield. Elizabeth and Greenwood Bell had 13 children (including four sets of twins) in 22 years. If these dates are accurate, Elizabeth Roll's youngest child was born when she was 45 years of age:

    I.   Arthur (b. November 13, 1810; d. October 12, 1872)

    II.   Mary Elizabeth (b. December 1, 1812; d. January 16, 1887) married William McCracken

    III. Delilah (b. June 29, 1815; d. August 3, 1841)

    IV.   David (b. June 29, 1815)

    V.   John (b. July 6, 1819; d. October 7, 1848)

    VI.   William (b. July 6, 1819; d. March 20, 1877)

    VII. Julian (b. September 24, 1821)

    VIII. Julia A. (b. September 24, 1821; d. August 22, 1824)

    IX.   David Roll (b. February 11, 1824; d. December 31, 1875)

X.   Margaret (b. December 29, 1925; d. January 11, 1911)

XI.   Grier (b. March 17, 1827; d. 1898)

XII.   Harvey (b. March 17, 1827; d. March 13, 1831)

XIII.   Frampton (b. August 31, 1832; d. April 2, 1910)

David Roll Bell (5ᵗʰ generation) married **Margery Hoover (5ᵗʰ generation)** and are the parents of Mary Erie Bell **(6ᵗʰ generation)**. (Return to page 69 @ Mary Erie Bell to rejoin the Maternal Lineage for Howard Jefferson Thompson, Part I.)

i   Completely a supposition on part of the author, but Ann's second name of Kinta or her third name of Cunigunda could possibly be her maiden name suggesting that she also may have been widowed (married name of Hoffman) and had had children in an earlier marriage at an earlier age.

ii   Other sources give the date of 1869 and one source has the date as 1892.

iii   The fact of this birth was new information to me as of September 2015, with the only record being a tombstone; however, the Fleming Family Tree identifies baby Erie as female.

iv   The details are included here because Walter left Curwensville and never returned. We Thompson sisters did not know there was a great-uncle Walter or that our father had a cousin Irene.

v   Fred's children were Frederick, Mary Elizabeth, Jane, and Maud Ann.

vi   Francis' children were Darl Francis, Robert Walter, Lois May, and William Lee.

vii   William, the youngest of this generation of Thompson siblings and cousins, was a well-known designer of period rooms, particularly those in New York City mansions and Southern plantations owned by Richard Jenrette, Bill's life partner and a well-known financier, who collected and restored antebellum residences. Bill's work was featured at the Antiques Show in the NYC Armory in the 1990s (which Judith attended). He and Jenrette divided their time among Charleston, SC, a New York City brownstone, Edgewater, once owned by Gore Vidal, in Watertown, NY, and other properties. Bill has authored *Beginnings* and *Ghostly Poems*. Richard Jenrette's book *Adventures with Old Houses* includes a foreword by the Prince of Wales with whom Mr. Jenrette has interests in common.

viii   There is a possibility that this child's birth and death date is wrong here and that the death in infancy is Baby Erie born/died in 1872. I have not been able to confirm this.

ix   There is an egregious error of the birth date on Elizabeth's tombstone as 1881; ALL records, including her obituary, use the correct date of 1880. This mistake was very upsetting to Howard, Jr. who could not believe that his father would not correct the error on the stone.

x   In 1948 Bill Jackson was legally adopted by Bradford B. Crunk, but retained (at Mr. Crunk's insistence) the name of his birth father "to always honor him," as Brad noted.

Paternal Lineage

for

Elizabeth Bailey Spencer Thompson

Paternal Lineage for Elizabeth Bailey Spencer Thompson

"The Spencers"

The following is an account of the paternal lineage of Elizabeth Bailey Spencer Thompson, the paternal grandmother of Kay, Judith, Jo Ellen, and Nan Thompson. As many of the records for Joseph Smith did not use "Senior" or "Junior" designations (and in some cases designated in error), the lineage below cannot be confirmed as exact.

1st generation (dates align with the 2nd generation of the John Pifer Paternal Lineage)

The first trace of this Spencer line in America is of **Samuel Bond Spencer** (son of Samuel Spencer and Elizabeth Bond) who likely was born in England in 1728 and immigrated to America. He married **Hannah Boyd** (b. in Montgomery in 1731; d. September 9, 1796[i]), the daughter of John Boyd and Hannah Powell Bell.[ii] Samuel died in Montgomery County on September 9, 1796.

Samuel Bond Spencer and Hannah Boyd were married on April 14, 1751 and are the parents of the following children:[iii]

    I.   **Joseph** (b. 1752; d. February 4, 1832 [or July 11, 1831]) **(2nd)**

    II.   John (b. January 23, 1754; d. January 22, 1829)

    III.   Mary Spencer (b. 1756; d. 1826)

    IV.   Infant (female) (b. 1758)

2nd generation (dates align with the 3rd generation of the John Pifer Paternal Lineage)

This "first" **Joseph Spencer** was born in Chester County in 1752 and died February 4, 1832. In 1780 he married **(Ann) Nancy Tompkins** (b. 1760 in Centre County; d. February 11, 1859). Shortly after their marriage they likely moved to Centre County, as this is listed as the birthplace of their first born son Joseph, Jr. The family later moved to the Grampian area of Clearfield County.

"Among the adult men who came to the Clearfield-Curwensville-Grampian area between 1808 and 1813 is listed a **Joseph Spencer** who settled in the Grampian Hills of Pennsylvania around 1818 when he purchased 440 acres between Pennsville (Grampian) and the Susquehanna River. He divided that land into four farms, one for himself and the others for his three sons.[iv]"

The following (possibly) are the children of Joseph Spencer and (Ann) Nancy Tompkins[v]:

    I.   Samuel (b. 1783; d. June 1854 in Clearfield) married Sarah

    II.   **Joseph** (Jr.) (b. July 13, 1784 [or 1787] in Half Moon Valley, Centre County; d. July 24 [or December 24], 1857) **(3rd)**

III.   Hannah (b. 1788; d. 1856 in Clearfield)

IV.   Nancy (b. 1790; d. June 1854[59])

V.   Jesse Fisher (b. November 28, 1793 in Centre County; d. March 28, 1876 in Clearfield), married Anna Moore

VI.   (Martha) Patty (b. 1795; d. April 3, 1825 in Clearfield)

3rd generation (dates align with the 4th generation of the John Pifer Paternal Lineage)

Joseph Spencer, Jr. (b. July 13, 1784 [or 1787]: d. July 24, 1857) married **Lydia Moore** (b. January 22, 1790 in Lancaster; d. January 15, 1873 in Grampian Hills). Lydia Moore's parents were Lydia Sharpless and James Moore.

Joseph Spencer, Jr. married Lydia Moore on August 8, 1811 in Grampian, Pennsylvania. They are the parents of the following children:

I.   Charles (b. July 19, 1812 in Clearfield; d. April 7, 1835 in An, Rakhine State, Myanmar, Asia) (Might he have been a Quaker missionary?)

II.   James (b. October 1, 1813 in Penn Township, Pennsylvania; d. January 14, 1864)

III.   Samuel (b. November 12, 1815 in Penn Township; d. September 5, 1865 in Clearfield); married Lydia Bell (b. 1820; d. 1856)

IV.   Nancy (b. May 22, 1817 in Bridgeport; d. October 17, 1861 in Clearfield); married William Smith Porter (b. 1816; d. 1855)

V.   Martha (b. February 28, 1819 in Penn Township; d. 1863 in Medina, Ohio); married Theodore D. England (b. 1817; b. 1862)

VI.   **Joseph Moore** (b. March 31, 1821; d. July 26, 1889 [or 82] in Curwensville) (4th)

VII.   Lavinia (b. January 31, 1823 in Penn Township; d. September 27, 1851 in Clearfield)

VIII. Miles Sharpless (b. November 13, 1824 in Penn Township; d. August 11, 1900) married Lucinda Griest

IX.   Eliza (b. December 22, 1828 in Penn Township; d. March 10, 1876 in Clearfield); married Cabel Way Moore (b. 1926)

X.   Harrison Wayne (b. August 21, 1832 in Grampian; d. August 27, 1906 in Curwensville); married Amanda M. Garretson (b. 1835; d. 1902)

4th generation (dates align with the 5th generation of the John Pifer Paternal Lineage)

Joseph Moore Spencer (b. March 31, 1821; d. July 26, 1889) is described as a leading member of the Quaker sect, of kindly disposition,[v] charitable, and an ideal citizen in every respect.[vi]

Lydia Ann Griest (b. April 20, 1820; d. September 27, 1882) lived in York County, two hundred miles from Grampian. In 1843 Lydia, whose parents were Uriah Griest (b. June 29, 1789; d. September 15, 1851) and Margaret Mary Vale (b. May 5, 1794; d. January 21, 1854), came to the Grampian area to visit with her Aunt Ruth, who recently had married a widower, Gideon Widemire. It was there that Lydia first met Joseph Moore Spencer.

Both Joseph and Lydia were Quakers and they began a four-year, long-distance courtship through correspondence. These letters later were transcribed as a booklet by their great grandsons ("A Quaker Courtship in the 1840s"). In one of her letters, Lydia described her father as one "(who) owns no land, yet he is much respected … has made an honest living, mostly on the loom."[vii]

Joseph's intermittent ill health during the long period of their friendship kept the young couple from meeting face to face, except for a few times during their courtship. In fact, doubts about Joseph's recovery from his long-term illness nearly terminated their relationship.

Finally, after a written proposal, hesitation, and then mutual acceptance, Joseph and Lydia were married at the Huntington Meeting House in Adams County on January 25, 1849. "It was mid-winter, no cars, no trains, no good roads. Just horses and sleigh."[viii]

Joseph M. Spencer and Lydia Griest are the parents of the following children, all born in Bridgeport, Clearfield County:

    I.   Lavinia (b. June 25, 1851; died August 28, 1871 of consumption)

    II.   **Vincent Uriah** (b. May 14, 1854; d. January 12, 1950) (5th)

    III.   Roland Jesse (b. January 7, 1857; d. December 20, 1928 in Ashland, Oregon)

    IV.   Almina Jane (b. January 12, 1859; lived past the age of 100.[ix]) Almina and her husband Joseph J. Downing had two daughters:

        I. Della Mae (b. 1884)

        II. Ada Irene (b. 1889)

    V.   *Jane (dates unknown. It is also possible that the reference was intended for Almina Jane.)*[x]

    VI.   Amos (dates unknown, so the birth order here is unconfirmed, and there is no confirmation of this name in Ancestry.com, although it is noted in family records.)

Joseph M. Spencer ran a farm as well as operating a grist mill and is said to have built one of the first homes in Bridgeport, into which he and his bride settled. In addition to farming, Joseph taught school in the original one-room school near the Grampian Quaker Meeting House (which explains why he was later comfortable serving in his daughter Lavinia's stead when she was ill during the last year of her short life and not strong enough to teach at her own school.)

5th generation (dates align with the 6th generation of the John Pifer Paternal Lineage)

Vincent Uriah Spencer (b. May 14, 1854; d. January 12, 1950) lived in Bridgeport, which was at that time a busy commercial community of several hundred residents. When Vincent was not working in his father's grist mill, he joined the work of hauling timber out of the woods to Anderson Creek. He once rode one of the rafts (used for transporting the lumber) as far as Jersey Shore, Pennsylvania. During his lifetime Vincent made three overland trips to the West Coast, perhaps to visit his brother Roland).

Vincent U. Spencer attended a college in Poughkeepsie, New York for at least a year, and at the age of 19 began a career of more than 20 years of teaching. He likely attended summer sessions of the Curwensville Academy, a Normal School which offered courses intended to prepare teachers. Vincent's years of teaching included service in schools at Grampian, Chestnut Ridge, Locust Ridge, Bridgeport, and Pike Township. He later served as a school director in Pike Township and Curwensville Borough.

Vincent U. Spencer also followed the mercantile business for a number of years until the decline of Bridgeport as a commercial community with its woolen mills and other small industries began, following the devastating Johnstown Flood of 1889. At that time Anderson Creek, near Bridgeport, went on a rampage and caused overwhelmingly destructive damage to many homes and other buildings in the lowlands.

With this change in his community, Vincent looked for new opportunities and became interested in developing and installing electrical units in the towns and villages in Centre and other nearby counties. This is possibly when he became acquainted with the Thompson brothers who also shared this business interest.

As was custom with many young women, Lavinia Spencer, Vincent's older sister, kept a diary. What was not usual, however, is that Lavinia's diary ended with her death in 1871 at age 20 from consumption. During the last, sad year of her life both Vincent and their father frequently took Lavinia's place teaching in her one-room school when she was too ill to leave the house. In a time without drugs or a defined medical treatment, Lavinia's father searched for any cure or alleviation of her illness, but to no avail.[xi]

> - May 19, 1871. "Papa came up to my room this morning and talked to me a while. He is thinking some of writing to doctor in New York. Feel weaker than yesterday."
>
> - May 22, 1871. "Got a box of pills from Philadelphia. Papa sent for them last sixth day."

The younger of Vincent's two sisters, Almina Spencer, married Joseph J. Downing on May 10, 1883; the Downings settled in Xenia, Ohio. In 1959 a local newspaper article announced the celebration of Almina Spencer Downing's 100th birthday in Xenia (see *The Story of Kate and Howard*[xii]).

Vincent Uriah Spencer (b. May 14, 1854; d. January 12, 1950) married **Mary Alice Bailey** (b. April 16, 1854; d. July 19, 1937).

It is at this point that the Spencer and Bailey families were joined.

Vincent Uriah Spencer and Mary Alice Bailey were married on October 1 (or 2), 1878 and are the parents of two daughters, born 14 months apart:

    I.   Grace Cecilia (b. July 17, 1879 in Bridgeport; d. June 22, 1944, in Clearfield)

    II.   **Elizabeth Bailey** (born September 14, 1880 in Bridgeport; d. October 10, 1951 in Clearfield) (6th)

6th **generation** (dates align with the 7th generation of the John Pifer Paternal Lineage)

Elizabeth Bailey Spencer (b. September 14, 1880; d. October 10, 1951) married **Howard Jefferson Thompson** (b. January 12, 1878; d. January 3, 1968), son of Francis Ignatius Thompson and Mary Erie Bell.

The marriage of Elizabeth Bailey Spencer and Howard J. Thompson links the Maternal and Paternal Lineages of Elizabeth and Howard J.

The wedding of Elizabeth Bailey Spencer and Howard Jefferson Thompson was held the morning of June 17, 1903 in the home of the bride's parents.[xiii] Elizabeth and Howard are the parents of the following children:

I.   **Howard Vincent** (b. April 10, 1904 in Clearfield; d. January 14, 1964 in Clearfield) (7th) (see progeny below)

II.   Mary Alice (b. November 21, 1905 in Clearfield; d. April 19, 1998 in State College) first married William Kitson Jackson (b. December 28, 1906; d. February 23, 1945, a WWII casualty at Henri-Chapelle, Belgium). On December 28, 1946 Mary Alice married Bradford Blueford Crunk (b. February 16, 1914 in Lockhart, Texas; d. May 1, 1998 in State College). Mary Alice and William Jackson are the parents of one child:

William Spencer Jackson (b. September 4, 1934 in Philadelphia)[xiv]; married Rosemary Keating in 1960. They are the parents of two children:

I.   Tracy (Chloe Valeria and Kyleigh Rose)

II.   William Kitson II (Sage Marie and Kitson)

III.   Philip Bell (b. October 20, 1919 in Bellefonte; d. January 21, 2001 in Altoona) married Eva Hart (b. June 15, 1922; d. September 4, 2010) circa 1951. They are the parents of two children:

I.   Patricia Ann (b. April 25, 1952; d. December 17, 2008)

II.   Mark Allen (Jessica Sue Walters and Morgan Rae), Williamsburg, Virginia as of 2008

Howard Jefferson Thompson, known as H. J., was engaged in various successful businesses—water, electricity, coal, movie theatres, a knitting mill, and banking. He was president of the Cassidy Coal Company, Central Penn Light and Power Company, Curwensville Water Company, Curwensville State Bank, and Mid State Theatres, as well as co-owner of the knitting mill. Some would have called him the second Fred Dyer. He also ran twice for a seat in the Pennsylvania State Senate. Those who knew him would have described H. J. as "a hard man." Elizabeth shared in the ownership of the Mid State Theatres, retaining (protecting) her shares for her children.

7th generation (dates align with the 8th generation of the John Pifer Paternal Lineage)

Howard Vincent Thompson, whose sister gave him the nickname "Bubby," was born in Clearfield, then moved to East Linn Street in Bellefonte after the age of six. The family later returned to Clearfield circa 1921. Bubby worked for his father most of his life, beginning in his early teens, reading meters, installing meters, and trimming street arcs. After attending Williamsport Business College, he served as secretary and treasurer of the Curwensville Water Company from 1925 until 1941 at which time he became manager of the Rex Theatre. In addition, he was a former Curwensville Borough tax collector, auditor, and minority inspector of the election board in Curwensville's First Ward. He later served as president of Mid State Theatres. He also was very active in Volunteer Firemen's Associations, the Loyal Order of Moose, and the IOOF.

Howard Vincent Thompson (b. April 10, 1904 in Clearfield; d. January 14, 1964 in Clearfield) married **Katherine Shields Pifer** (b. February 11, 1908 in Curwensville; d. January 31, 1998 in Hershey), daughter of John and Matilda Smith Pifer.

Catherine S. Pifer (as her name appears on the marriage license)[xv] and Howard V. Thompson, Jr.[xvi] were married on June 20, 1927 in Clearfield; the date was the 33rd wedding anniversary of her parents' marriage. Catherine and Howard are the parents of four daughters:

    I.   **Matilda Kay** (b. November 1, 1930 in Curwensville) **(8th)**

    II.   **Judith Evelyn** (b. March 9, 1937 in Clearfield) **(8th)**

    III.   **Jo Ellen** (b. November 6, 1938 in Clearfield) **(8th)**

    IV.   **Elizabeth Nan** (b. August 19, 1942 in Clearfield) **(8th)**

8th generation (dates align with the 9th generation of the John Pifer Paternal Lineage)

It was this generation who moved from Curwensville, each in turn after high school graduation: Kay moving to California, but returning to Curwensville in the late 1980s; Judith settling in Hummelstown, Pennsylvania to teach in the newly formed Lower Dauphin Junior-Senior High School; Jo Ellen leaving for government service and later working in her husband's CPA firm in the DC area; and Nan to DC, then California, returning to live in Hershey, Pennsylvania, where she worked in public relations and publications for the Penn State Medical Center, now as designer for Yesteryear Publishing.

At this point the genealogies merge and become one with the Thompson Sisters who originate through the marriage of Catherine Pifer and Howard V. Thompson.

As explained in the section on the Paternal Lineage of John Frederick Pifer, which was used as the baseline, the genealogies are aligned by the ages of those who lived at a common time. Because a lineage begins with the first generation of a family that could be found, a person identified in the third generation of one lineage might match in age to those in the sixth generation of another's lineage. For example, in this set of genealogies, persons named in the seventh generation of Elizabeth's Paternal Lineage, would match in age with those in the eighth generation of John Pifer's Maternal Lineage as well as in his Paternal Lineage because his ancestors on both sides (mother and father) are of the same timeframe (similar birth dates).

Most frequently a person appears in different generations in the separate lineages. For example, because Matilda Pifer's mother's lineage could not be traced back very many generations (There are no records for the key people), Catherine and Howard Thompson are only the third generation in her Maternal Lineage, but are eighth in John Pifer's Maternal Lineage—or even 27th if we count the lineage back to William the Conqueror.

To demonstrate, those of the 1st generation of Matilda Smith Pifer's Maternal Lineage would align with the following:

- 4th generation of her own Paternal Lineage
- 4th generation of H. J. Thompson's Paternal Lineage
- 5th generation of Elizabeth Spencer Thompson's Paternal Lineage
- 6th generation of Elizabeth's Maternal Lineage and of H. J.'s Maternal Lineage
- 6th generation of John F. Pifer's Maternal Lineage and Paternal Lineage beginning in America or the 25th generation (if we include to William the Conqueror) of his Maternal Lineage

THE THOMPSON SISTERS ARE

9th generation of Howard Jefferson Thompson's Maternal Lineage
7th generation of his Paternal Lineage

9th generation of Elizabeth Spencer Thompson's Maternal Lineage
8th generation of her Paternal Lineage

9th (or 28th if we include back to William the Conqueror) generation of John Frederick Pifer's Maternal Lineage
9th generation of his Paternal Lineage

4th generation of Matilda Smith Pifer's Maternal Lineage
7th generation of her Paternal Lineage

Matilda Kay

Following graduation Kay, a talented dancer, went to Philadelphia and auditioned for a place in a music hall/theatre chorus line. After a year in Philadelphia and being wooed by the man "back home," she returned to Curwensville. However, the call of far-away places led her to leave her hometown for California where she worked for Pacific Mutual and about a year later found her dream job with Trans World Airlines.

On August 26, 1950 Matilda Kay Thompson married Albert R. Brunetti (born June 12, 1924; d. August 19, 2012; son of Oreste and Edith Durandetto Brunetti). They are the parents of one child, a daughter, Mavis Kim, born on September 2, 1952. Following a divorce from Albert Brunetti, years later on May 22, 1980 Kay married **Robert A. Walker** of Clearfield.

The child of Kay Thompson and Albert Brunetti

> **Mavis Kim** (b. September 2, 1952 in Clearfield) (9th)

9th generation (dates align with the 9th generation of the John Pifer Paternal Lineage)

Kim Richards lives in Cathedral City, California and is based in Palm Springs where she is a Buyer and Personal Shopper for Macy's. In 1970 Kim married Earl Richards, but the marriage later ended in divorce.

Judith Evelyn

Judith holds an earned doctorate in administration; served as a high school English teacher, principal, and assistant to the superintendent; worked for the Pennsylvania Department of Education; and is the Director of the Capital Area Institute for Mathematics and Science at Penn State Harrisburg. She also heads a private consulting business (Educon) and a publishing company (Yesteryear Publishing). In addition, she has chaired a number of major civic events and is the author of eighteen books, many on social history.

On September 6, 1958 **Judith Evelyn Thompson** (b. March 9, 1937) married **Thomas Eugene Ball** (b. January 31, 1937), son of Elmer and Rena Graham Ball. Following a divorce, on February 25, 1972 Judith married **Walter C. Witmer** (b. January 18, 1931; d. June 13, 2003), son of Miles and Ethel Espenshade Witmer).

The children of Judith Thompson and Thomas Ball

> I. **Jean Rochelle Ball** (b. March 7, 1959 in Harrisburg) (9th)
> II. **Thomas Ross Ball** (b. April 23, 1968 in Camp Hill) (9th)

9th generation (dates align with the 9th generation of the John Pifer Paternal Lineage)

Jean Rochelle Ball Jacobs is the staff accountant for Kurtz Bros. in Clearfield, Pennsylvania. She married James Gary Jacobs (b. October 3, 1948) in 1984.

The children of Jean Rochelle Ball and James Jacobs

> I. **Jordan Ashlee** (b. April 17, 1986 in Clearfield) (10th)
> II. **Jillian Rochelle** (b. October 29, 1992 in Clearfield) (10th)

Thomas Ross Ball is the owner of Thomas Ball Entertainment in Hershey, Pennsylvania. He married **Michelle Ann Garger** (b. 1971) in 2000; they were divorced in 2015. The children of Thomas Ross Ball and Michelle Garger

> I. **Emily Madison** (b. July 11, 2002 in Harrisburg) (10th)
> II. **Olivia Emerson** (b. June 27, 2005 in Harrisburg) (10th)

10th generation (dates align with the 9th generation of the John Pifer Paternal Lineage)

As of September 2015:

> **Jordan Ashlee Jacobs** is employed by Laborers Int'l. Union of North America 158 HCL.
>
> **Jillian Rochelle Jacobs** is Hospital Operations Coordinator for United Health Services.
>
> **Emily Madison Ball** is in eighth grade at the Lower Dauphin Middle School.
>
> **Olivia Emerson Ball** is in fifth grade at Conewago Elementary School.

Jo Ellen

Jo Ellen began her professional career with the Federal Bureau of Investigation (FBI) in Washington, DC, followed by a position with the National Security Agency (the top intelligence organization of the U.S. government), then the newest government agency—later to become the premium agency with the highest clearances required—where she quickly earned a high-level administrative position. She later joined her husband in his business, Lorenz and Lorenz Certified Public Accountants.

On September 6, 1958, in a double wedding with her sister Judith, **Jo Ellen Thompson** (b. November 6, 1938) married **Eugene Kendall Lorenz** (b. September 19, 1932), the son of Alma ("Bonnie") Corinne Miller and Eugene Hurdle Lorenz.

The children of Jo Ellen Thompson and Eugene Kendall Lorenz

> I.   **Janelle Corinne Lorenz Wright** (b. January 2, 1969) (9th)
>
> II. **Eugene Kendall Lorenz, Jr.** (b. April 17, 1970; d. January 3, 2013) (9th)

9th generation (dates align with the 9th generation of the John Pifer Paternal Lineage)

Janelle Lorenz Wright manages real estate for her parents and her family. Previously, she was employed by KPMG Peat Marwick and as the private label buyer for Saks Fifth Avenue's catalog division.

Janelle Lorenz married **Jay Oscar Wright** (b. December 12, 1969, St. Johnsbury, Vermont) on October 25, 1997. They reside in Potomac, Maryland. They are the parents of

> I.   **Corinne Catherine Wright** (b. May 29, 2001 in Sarasota, Florida) (10th)
>
> II. **Theodore Piers Wright** (b. September 30, 2002 in Silver Spring, Maryland) (10th)

10th generation (dates align with the 9th generation of the John Pifer Paternal Lineage)

As of September 2015:

> **Corinne Catherine Wright** is in the ninth grade at The Connelly School of the Holy Child, Potomac, Maryland.
>
> **Theodore Piers Wright** is in the sixth grade at Echelon Academy, Sandy Spring, Maryland.

Elizabeth Nan

Nan began her professional career with the National Security Agency in Washington, DC. She later moved to Southern California where she worked for the City of Anaheim. Following a return to Pennsylvania, she worked in Development for Dickinson College in Carlisle before finding her niche in Public Relations for Penn State's College of Medicine and Hershey Medical Center. Currently she manages and is the page designer for Yesteryear Publishing.

On August 18, 1965 **Elizabeth Nan Thompson** (b. August 19, 1942) married **Joel Keith Edmunds** (b. August 14, 1942), the son of Irvin C. and Jaclyn Beck Edmunds.

The children of Elizabeth Nan Thompson and Joel Keith Edmunds

    I.   **Shayne Scott Edmunds** (b. December 9, 1965 in Northridge, California) (9th)

    II. **Jesse Joel Edmunds** (b. November 6, 1979 in Lucerne Valley, California) (9th)

9th generation (dates align with the 9th generation of the John Pifer Paternal Lineage)

Shayne Edmunds and his wife, **Grace Graybill,** are co-owners of the Neato Burrito restaurant chain located throughout South Central Pennsylvania.

Shayne Edmunds married **Ada Grace Graybill** (b. November 10, 1969) on June 15, 1999. They reside in Dillsburg, Pennsylvania and are the parents of

    I.   **Aero Graham** (b. April 18, 2004 in Harrisburg, Pennsylvania) (10th)

    II. **Iris Isadora** (b. September 2, 2005 in Harrisburg, Pennsylvania) (10th)

Jesse Edmunds is an outdoor adventurer as well as an accomplished musician who currently performs in the Greater Harrisburg, Pennsylvania area. He resides in Hershey, Pennsylvania.

10th generation (dates align with the 9th generation of the John Pifer Paternal Lineage)

As of September 2015:

    Aero Graham is in the sixth grade at Northern Middle School in Dillsburg, Pennsylvania.

    Iris Isadora is in the fifth grade at Northern Elementary School in Dillsburg, Pennsylvania.

[i]   It is puzzling that the death date of Samuel and Hannah Boyd Spencer is the same. Perhaps this is in error for one of them.

[ii]   Dates not verified; date of birth for Hannah is given as 1751, the same as her year of marriage and therefore cannot be accurate. Perhaps her date of birth is 1731, rather than 1751.

[iii] Ancesty.com lists Nathan Spence, born 1731, as a child of Hannah and Samuel. I did not include this because I think it is an error.

[iv]   "Early History," *150th Anniversary,* Curwensville, PA, 1949, p. 11.

[v]   There are several questionable dates for the family of Joseph Spencer and (Ann) Nancy Tompkins. There may have been two families with similar names. Rather than exclude, I have elected to include any of the possibilities for these offspring.

[vi]   Lavinia in her Diary mentions her father several times; a kindly man who tried to find remedies for her illness, including writing to a physician in another state.

[vii] Straw, Albert Y. *Some Genealogies and Family Records, 1931*: Press of Clearfield Republican.

[viii] From letters written to Joseph, collected in "A Quaker Courtship in the 1840s," compiled by the Wall brothers, sons of Charles and Grace Wall.

[ix]   Ibid, containing the description presented by their son Vincent at the 100th Anniversary of the West Branch Friends Meeting, Grampian, in 1933.

[x]   This disproves the date of death given in Ancestry.com

[xi]   The birth of this child is not confirmed, only indicated by one of the sources used for this information.

[xii] Judith was given the diary of her great-grand-aunt, Lavinia (sometimes spelled Lavina).

[xiii] Published by Yesteryear Publishing, 2015.

[xiv] The account of this wedding is in a book, a wedding gift from Grace to her sister Elizabeth.

[xv]   In 1948 Bill Jackson was legally adopted by Bradford B. Crunk, but retained (at Mr. Crunk's insistence) the name of his birth father "to always honor him," as Brad noted.

[xvi] Mother told us that this is the spelling Howard used and she continued with it.

[xvii] Howard used the "Jr." designation even though his middle name was not that of his father.

Maternal Lineage

for

Elizabeth Bailey Spencer Thompson

Maternal Lineage for Elizabeth Bailey Spencer Thompson

"The Baileys"

The following is an account of the maternal lineage of Elizabeth Bailey Spencer Thompson, the paternal grandmother of Kay, Judith, Jo Ellen, and Nan Thompson.

Information for the Baileys includes that they were of English descent and immigrated to the American Colonies before the Revolutionary War. They were Quakers and were likely influenced in coming to this country by William Penn who founded the colony of Pennsylvania.

Newer information (September 2015) provides ancestry beginning in England with the birth of **William Brinton** (b. December 1, 1636 in Sedgeley Parish, Staffordshire, England; d. 1700 in Birmingham, Chester, Pennsylvania). He married **Ann Bagley** (b. in 1635, also in Staffordshire, England; d. in Birmingham, Chester, Pennsylvania). It is likely William and Ann knew each other in childhood, married, and immigrated to America sometime after the birth of their daughter **Elizabeth** (b. 1670; d. October 27, 1715 in Sedgley, Staffordshire). Both parents (William and Ann Brinton) died some years later in Chester, Pennsylvania. This, then, makes them the first generation in America, but **not** the first to be born here.

Elizabeth Brinton married **Hugh Harry** who was born in 1660 in Machynlleth, Montgomeryshire, Wales and died in 1708; this indicates that both Elizabeth Brinton and Hugh Harry were born in the British Isles. They are the parents of **Olive Harry** (b. 1703; d. October 4, 1766 in Birmingham). (Hugh Harry likely had immigrated to America where he met his first wife and started his first family. It is also likely then that Elizabeth Brinton also came to America but perhaps returned to England before her death which reportedly was in Staffordshire.)

There is mention of Olive Harry's half-sister, Elizabeth Harry (1694-1758). The following listing may be the first family of Hugh Harry before he married Elizabeth Brinton or they **more likely are** the children of Hugh and Elizabeth Brinton Harry, with Olive being the half-sister. The information this is based on was inconclusive and, at times, misleading.

- Evan Harry, 1687–1728 (Birmingham)
- William, 1689
- Hugh, 1690–1760
- Jane, 1690–1743
- John, 1692
- Elizabeth, 1694–1758
- Lois, 1699–1699

Thus, the following becomes the first generation born in America and aligns with the 1st generation of the John Pifer Paternal Lineage.

Olive Harry (b. 1703; d. October 4, 1766) married **Daniel Bailey** (b. December 3, 1693 in Chester County, Pennsylvania; d. 1783 in East Marlborough, Pennsylvania).

Olive Harry and Daniel Bailey were married on January 16, 1720 in Goshen, Chester County, Pennsylvania. They are the parents of the following children:

- William (b. December 9, 1721; d. 1783)
- Ann (b. March 6, 1722; d. 1810)
- Elizabeth (b. October 16, 1725; d. 1818 in Delaware or Chester County)
- **Daniel Bailey** (b. January 21, 1731; d. November 11, 1810) **(2nd)**
- Lydia Bailey (b. March 27, 1734)
- Olive Bailey (b. February 14, 1735)
- Claudius (b. February 14, 1737; d. 1794)
- Caleb (b. April 14, 1738; d. 1794)
- Nathan (b. November 10, 1744) *(Note the gap in years between the births of Caleb and Nathan which is observed in many of the lineages where the last child born is some years younger than the preceding sibling.)*

2nd generation (dates align with the 2nd generation of the John Pifer Paternal Lineage)

Daniel Bailey (b. January 21, 1731 in East Marlborough, Chester County, Pennsylvania; d. November 11, 1810 in Loyalsock, Lycoming County, Pennsylvania) married **Ann Wakefield** (b. April 21, 1731 in Somerset County [?]; died 1795 in Lycoming County).

Daniel Bailey and Ann Wakefield were married on September 24, 1755 in Fairfax County, Virginia. They are the parents of the following children:

I. Ann (b. 1756; d. 1844)

II. Olive (b. 1757; likely died in infancy since a later child bears the same name)

III. Infant daughter (b. August 21, 1758; d. August 23, 1758)

IV. Caleb (b. September 3, 1759 in Clearfield [or on April 3 in Chester County, based on earlier DAR history]; d. December 9, 1840 in Pike Township, Clearfield County) **(3rd)**

V. Nathan (b. August 5, 1761)

VI. Wakefield (b. August 5, 1761) (Nathan and Wakefield are twins.)

VII. Daniel (b. August 29, 1763)

VIII. Olive (b. 1765)

IX. Harry (no dates, but listed as a child, following the birth of Olive)

3rd generation (dates align with the 3rd generation of the John Pifer Paternal Lineage)

Caleb Bailey (b. April 3, 1759 in Chester County or September 3 in Clearfield County; d. December 9, 1840 in Pike Township, Clearfield County) married Elizabeth Harry (b. June 27, 1764 in Chester County; d. December 31, 1853/54 in Clearfield County).

Caleb Bailey and Elizabeth Harry were married on March 6, 1787. They are the parents of the following children:

I. Reuben (b. January 4, 1788; d. April 22, 1788)

II. Eliza (b. January 1, 1789; d. February 14, 1813 in Curwensville)

III. Margaret (b. July 26, 1791 in Chester County; d. April 5, 1853 in Clearfield County)

IV. Ann (b. May 17, 1793; d. January 16, 1825)

V. **Daniel** (b. July 31, 1795 in Curwensville; d. August 7, 1875) **(4th)**

VI. Caleb, Jr. (b. September 27, 1797 in Lycoming County; d. November 29, 1885 in Luthersburg) married Jemina Sunderland

VII. Charlotte (b. January 15, 1800; d. 1830)

VIII. Elizabeth (b. January 22, 1802 in Clearfield County; d. 1842)

IX. Titus Henry (b. June 2, 1804 in Curwensville; d. 1866)

X. Nathan (b. December 25, 1806 in Curwensville; d. 1858)

XI. Jesse Kersey (b. December 25, 1808 in Curwensville; d. April 13, 1813)

Because Caleb, Jr. is the last of the children to be recorded as being born in Lycoming County and Elizabeth is the first registered as being born in Clearfield County, their father, Caleb, Sr., if not born in Clearfield County, may have moved from Lycoming between 1797 and 1802. He likely made the move with a group of other settlers, purchased a large tract of land on the ridge above Curwensville and began to clear a farm. Caleb Bailey, Sr. is named among those identified as "the earliest settlers in this part of Pennsylvania before December 1806."[i]

4th generation (dates align with the 4th generation of the John Pifer Paternal Lineage)

Daniel Bailey (b. July 31, 1795; d. August 7, 1875), second son (but first to reach adulthood) of Caleb Bailey, Sr. and Elizabeth Harry, married **Jane Passmore** (b. September 11, 1797 in Curwensville; d. August 30, 1877 in Curwensville). Jane was the daughter of Abraham Passmore (b. 1764; d. 1854) and Susanna Peirce (b. 1769; d. 1843).

Daniel Bailey and Jane Passmore were married on December 13, 1815. Daniel later purchased land covered with a stand of pine timber in the Pleasant Grove district in Pike Township. Later purchases expanded his land to four hundred acres.

The following are the children of Daniel and Jane Bailey:

I. *Maria (Mariah) (b. July 12, 1816; d. January 28, 1844) – not in Ancestry.com list*

II.   Isaac (b. February 17, 1818; d. December 16, 1851)

III.   Abraham Lincoln (b. November 17, 1819; d. December 16, 1904) married Jane

IV.   Mary Elizabeth (b. 1820; d. 1901)

V.   Joseph (b. March 5, 1823: d. October 19, 1902 [or September 7, 1901]) (5th)

VI.   Ann B. (b. April 8, 1825; d. January 7, 1900); married Jacob Anspach, August 1847

VII. Newton (b. February 7, 1827; possibly died very young since the last child in this family also was named Newton)

VIII. Ruth, likely a twin to Newton (b. February 7, 1827; d. January 18, 1847)

IX.   George (b. November 20, 1828; d. December 6, 1907)

X.   Calvin (b. July 26, 1831; d. September 7, 1907)

XI.   Levi (b. June 6, 1833; d. August 31, 1881)

XII. Harrison W. (b. July 17, 1835 or November 27, 1836 (date in Ancestry.com); d. May 10, 1896)

XIII. Lewis (b. January or June 28, 1838; died April 22, 1842)

XIV. Newton (b. April 16, 1841/42; d. March 26, 1867)

5th generation (dates align with the 5th generation of the John Pifer Paternal Lineage)

Joseph Bailey, (b. March [or May] 5, 1823 in Pike Township; d. September 7, 1901 [alternate date found of October 1902] in Lawrence Township) the third son of Daniel Bailey and Jane Passmore, married Sarah Elizabeth Boal (b. April 11, 1835; d. October 19, 1877). Sara Elizabeth's parents were James Boal (b. 1805; d. 1849) and Martha Ann Logue (b. 1805).

Joseph resided in Pike Township, near his father's homestead, engaging in lumbering and farming. He also owned several hundred acres of land, including what was known as the Bailey Homestead and later the Bailey Stone Quarry tract. H. J. Thompson later bought the Bailey land and the quarry.

Joseph Bailey and (Sarah) Elizabeth Boal (who lived in Centre County) were married on June 23, 1852. They are the parents of the following children:

I.   Mary Alice (b. April 16, 1854; d. July 19, 1937) (6th)

II.   Martha Jane (b. June 13, 1858/60; d. March 22, 1945). Martha Jane married Jonathan Ogden (b. 1856; d. 1928) of Clearfield in 1880.

III. James Dorsey (b. June/July, 1860; d. 1923)

IV. Annie G. (b. January 27, 1863; d. November 29, 1919) married Charles Boyd (Their son Russel married Mae Cora; thus, we now know the connection of Elizabeth Bailey Thompson to Mae Boyd at the theatre or perhaps water company office; they were cousins by marriage.)

V.   Charles C. (b. December 17, 1868; d. 1950)

6th generation (dates align with the 6th generation of the John Pifer Paternal Lineage)

(Mary) Alice Bailey (b. April 16, 1854 in Curwensville; d. July 19, 1937), daughter of Joseph Bailey and (Sarah) Elizabeth Boal, married **Vincent Uriah Spencer** (b. May 14, 1854; d. January 12, 1950), son of Joseph and Lydia Moore Spencer.

This marriage joined the Baileys and the Spencers, Elizabeth's maternal and paternal lines.

Vincent U. Spencer, a well-known citizen of Pike Township, was a leading member of the Quaker sect, described as "of kindly disposition, charitable spirit and an ideal citizen in every respect."[ii] Vincent followed the mercantile business for a number of years, later becoming interested in developing and installing electrical units in the towns and villages in Centre and other counties. (He also served as a school director and his signature appears on the diploma of Ruby Pifer, in the possession of the family.) Following the death of his wife, Mary Alice Bailey, Vincent made his home with his daughter Elizabeth and her husband H. J. Thompson.

Mary Alice Bailey and Vincent U. Spencer were married on October 2, 1878 and are the parents of two daughters:

    I.   Grace Cecilia (b. July 17, 1879 in Bridgeport; d. June 22, 1944, in Clearfield)

    II.   **Elizabeth Bailey** (b. September 14, 1880 in Bridgeport; d. October 10, 1951) **(7th)**

7th generation (dates align with the 7th generation of the John Pifer Paternal Lineage)

On June 11, 1902 Grace C. Spencer married Charles Miles Wall (b. November 30, 1877; d. October 26, 1945 as a result of a train accident in Carter, KY). Charles was the son of Miles Wall of Curwensville and an officer in the North American Refractories Company. He is numbered among the substantial business men of his generation. The family of Grace and Charles included the following children:

    I.   Charles Cecil (b. June 21, 1903 in Sadsbury, Lancaster, Pennsylvania; d. May 1, 1995) married Marguerite Thorp (b. May 15, 1908 in Curry Run; d. 1976.) (Marguerite's mother was Mary Jane Kerr and her father was "Rance" Thorp, also born in Curry Run.) In 1929 Cecil and Marguerite moved to Philadelphia, then to Alexandria, Virgina where Cecil served as the Resident Director of Mount Vernon). Cecil and Marguerite later moved to Greenwich, Connecticut where Cecil died.[iii] They were the parents of two daughters:

        1. Mary Jane married James McKean (McKean genealogy, Ancestry.com).
        2. Patricia Ann (b. 1935; d. 1969).

    II.   Marjorie Alice (b. June 4, 1905 in Curwensville; d. 1972 in Harrisburg)

    III.   Kenneth Spencer (b. February 12, 1908 in Curwensville; d. August 9, 1969) married Mauvis Fury of Bellefonte in 1930).

    IV.   Arthur Russel (b. May 16, 1920 in Curwensville; d. 2002 in Burlingame, California) married Gwendolyn Keith.

    V.   Richard Vincent (b. September 26/28, 1912/13 in Curwensville; d. September 25, 1992 in Boston, MA). Richard was married to Margaret and/or Rita and had one son, Richard.

Brothers Cecil and Ken were boyhood friends, as well as cousins, to Howard V., while Marjorie and Mary Alice were cousins as well as best girlhood friends.

Elizabeth Bailey Spencer (b. September 14, 1880; d. October 10, 1951) married **Howard Jefferson Thompson** (b. January 12, 1878; d. January 3, 1968), son of Francis Ignatius Thompson and Mary Erie Bell.

The marriage of Elizabeth Bailey Spencer and Howard J. Thompson links the Maternal and Paternal Lineages of Elizabeth and Howard J.

The wedding of Elizabeth Bailey Spencer and Howard Jefferson Thompson[iv] was held the morning of June 17, 1903 in the home of the bride's parents. Elizabeth and Howard are the parents of the following children:

    I.   **Howard Vincent** (b. April 10, 1904 in Clearfield; d. Jan. 14, 1964 in Clearfield) (8th) (see progeny below)

    II.   Mary Alice (b. November 21, 1905 in Clearfield; d. April 19, 1998 in State College) first married William Kitson Jackson (b. December 28, 1906; d. February 23, 1945, a WWII casualty at Henri-Chappelle, Belgium). On December 28, 1946 Mary Alice married Bradford Blueford Crunk (b. February 16, 1914 in Lockhart, Texas; d. May 1, 1998 in State College). Mary Alice and William Jackson are the parents of one child:

        William Spencer Jackson (b. September 4, 1934 in Philadelphia)[v]; married Rosemary Keating in 1960. They are the parents of two children:

            I. Tracy (Chloe Valeria and Kyleigh Rose)

            II. William Kitson II (Sage Marie and Kitson)

    III.   Philip Bell (b. October 20, 1919 in Bellefonte; d. January 21, 2001 in Altoona) married Eva Hart (b. June 15, 1922; d. September 4, 2010) circa 1951. They are the parents of two children:

        I. Patricia Ann (b. April 25, 1952; d. December 17, 2008)

        II. Mark Allen (Jessica Sue Walters and Morgan Rae), Williamsburg, Virginia as of 2008

Howard Jefferson Thompson, known as H. J., was engaged in various successful businesses—water, electricity, coal, movie theatres, a knitting mill, and banking. He was president of the Cassidy Coal Company, Central Penn Light and Power Company, Curwensville Water Company, Curwensville State Bank, and Mid State Theatres, as well as co-owner of the knitting mill. Some would have called him the second Fred Dyer. He also ran twice for a seat in the Pennsylvania State Senate. Those who knew him would have described H. J. as "a hard man." Elizabeth shared in the ownership of the Mid State Theatres, retaining (protecting) her shares for her children.

8th generation (dates align with the 8th generation of the John Pifer Paternal Lineage)

Howard Vincent Thompson, whose sister gave him the nickname "Bubby," was born in Clearfield, then moved to East Linn Street in Bellefonte after the age of six. The family later returned to Clearfield circa 1921. Bubby worked for his father most of his life, beginning in his early teens, reading meters, installing meters, and trimming street arcs. After attending Williamsport Business College, he served as secretary and treasurer of the Curwensville Water Company from 1925 until 1941 at which time he became manager of the Rex Theatre. In addition, he was a former Curwensville Borough tax collector, auditor, and minority inspector of the election board in Curwensville's First Ward. He later served as president of Mid State Theatres. He also was very active in Volunteer Firemen's Associations, the Loyal Order of Moose, and the IOOF.

Howard Vincent Thompson (b. April 10, 1904 in Clearfield; d. January 14, 1964 in Clearfield) married Katherine Shields Pifer (b. February 11, 1908 in Curwensville; d. January 31, 1998 in Hershey), daughter of John and Matilda Smith Pifer.

Catherine S. Pifer (as her name appears on the marriage license)[vi] and Howard V. Thompson, Jr.[vii] were married on June 20, 1927 in Clearfield; the date was the 33rd wedding anniversary of her parents' marriage. Catherine and Howard are the parents of the four daughters:

I.   Matilda Kay (b. November 1, 1930 in Curwensville) (9th)

II.   Judith Evelyn (b. March 9, 1937 in Clearfield) (9th)

III. Jo Ellen (b. November 6, 1938 in Clearfield) (9th)

IV. Elizabeth Nan (b. August 19, 1942 in Clearfield) (9th)

9th generation (dates align with the 9th generation of the John Pifer Paternal Lineage)

It was this generation who moved from Curwensville, each in turn after high school graduation: Kay moving to California, but returning to Curwensville in the late 1980s; Judith settling in Hummelstown, Pennsylvania to teach in the newly formed Lower Dauphin Junior-Senior High School; Jo Ellen leaving for government service, later working in her husband's CPA firm in the DC area; and Nan to DC, then California, returning to live in Hershey, Pennsylvania where she worked in public relations and publications for the Penn State Medical Center, now as designer for Yesteryear Publishing.

At this point the genealogies merge and become one with the Thompson Sisters who originate through the marriage of Catherine Pifer and Howard V. Thompson.

As explained in the section on the Paternal Lineage of John Frederick Pifer, which was used as the baseline, the genealogies are aligned by the ages of those who lived at a common time. Because a lineage begins with the first generation of a family that could be found, a person identified in the third generation of one lineage might match in age to those in the sixth generation of another's lineage. For example, in this set of genealogies, persons named in the seventh generation of Elizabeth's Paternal Lineage, would match in age with those in the eighth generation of John Pifer's Maternal Lineage as well as in his Paternal Lineage because his ancestors on both sides (mother and father) are of the same timeframe (similar birth dates).

Most frequently a person appears in different generations in the separate lineages. For example, because Matilda Pifer's mother's lineage could not be traced back very many generations (There are no records for the key people), Catherine and Howard Thompson are only the third generation in her Maternal Lineage, but are **eighth** in John Pifer's Maternal Lineage—or even **27**[th] if we count the lineage back to William the Conqueror.

To demonstrate, those of the **1**[st] **generation** of Matilda Smith Pifer's Maternal Lineage would align with the following:

- **4th generation** of her own Paternal Lineage

- **4th generation** of H. J. Thompson's Paternal Lineage

- **5th generation** of Elizabeth Spencer Thompson's Paternal Lineage

- **6th generation** of Elizabeth's Maternal Lineage and of H. J.'s Maternal Lineage

- **6th generation** of John F. Pifer's Maternal Lineage and Paternal Lineage beginning in America or the 25th generation (if we include to William the Conqueror) of his Maternal Lineage

THE THOMPSON SISTERS ARE

9th generation of Howard Jefferson Thompson's Maternal Lineage
7th generation of his Paternal Lineage

9th generation of Elizabeth Spencer Thompson's Maternal Lineage
8th generation of her Paternal Lineage

9th (or 28th if we include back to William the Conqueror) generation of John Frederick Pifer's Maternal Lineage
9th generation of his Paternal Lineage

4th generation of Matilda Smith Pifer's Maternal Lineage
7th generation of her Paternal Lineage

Matilda Kay

Following graduation Kay, a talented dancer, went to Philadelphia and auditioned for a place in a music hall/theatre chorus line. After a year in Philadelphia and being wooed by the man "back home," she returned to Curwensville. However, the call of far-away places led her to leave her hometown for California where she worked for Pacific Mutual and about a year later found her dream job with Trans World Airlines.

On August 26, 1950 **Matilda Kay Thompson** married **Albert R. Brunetti** (born June 12, 1924;

d. August 19, 2012; son of Oreste and Edith Durandetto Brunetti). They are the parents of one child, a daughter, Mavis Kim, born on September 2, 1952. Following a divorce from Albert Brunetti, years later on May 22, 1980 Kay married **Robert A. Walker** of Clearfield.

The child of Kay Thompson and Albert Brunetti

> **Mavis Kim** (b. September 2, 1952 in Clearfield) (10th)

10th generation (dates align with the 10th generation of the John Pifer Paternal Lineage)

Kim Richards lives in Cathedral City, California and is based in Palm Springs where she is a Buyer and Personal Shopper for Macy's. In 1970 Kim married Earl Richards, but the marriage later ended in divorce.

Judith Evelyn

Judith holds an earned doctorate in administration; served as a high school English teacher, principal, and assistant to the superintendent; worked for the Pennsylvania Department of Education; and is the Director of the Capital Area Institute for Mathematics and Science at Penn State Harrisburg. She also heads a private consulting business (Educon) and a publishing company (Yesteryear Publishing). In addition, she has chaired a number of major civic events and is the author of eighteen books, many on social history.

On September 6, 1958 **Judith Evelyn Thompson** (b. March 9, 1937) married **Thomas Eugene Ball** (b. January 31, 1937), son of Elmer and Rena Graham Ball. Following a divorce, on February 25, 1972 Judith married **Walter C. Witmer** (b. January 18, 1931; d. June 13, 2003), son of Miles and Ethel Espenshade Witmer).

The children of Judith Thompson and Thomas Ball

> I.   **Jean Rochelle Ball** (b. March 7, 1959 in Harrisburg) (10th)
>
> II.   **Thomas Ross Ball** (b. April 23, 1968 in Camp Hill) (10th)

10th generation (dates align with the 10th generation of the John Pifer Paternal Lineage)

Jean Rochelle Ball Jacobs is the staff accountant for Kurtz Bros. in Clearfield, Pennsylvania. She married James Gary Jacobs (b. October 3, 1948) in 1984.

The children of Jean Rochelle Ball and James Jacobs

> I.   **Jordan Ashlee** (b. April 17, 1986 in Clearfield) (11th)
>
> II.   **Jillian Rochelle** (b. October 29, 1992 in Clearfield) (11th)

Thomas Ross Ball is the owner of Thomas Ball Entertainment in Hershey, Pennsylvania. He married **Michelle Ann Garger** (b. 1971) in 2000; they were divorced in 2015. The children of Thomas Ross Ball and Michelle Garger

> I.   **Emily Madison** (b. July 11, 2002 in Harrisburg) (11th)
>
> II.   **Olivia Emerson** (b. June 27, 2005 in Harrisburg) (11th)

11th generation (dates align with the 11th generation of the John Pifer Paternal Lineage)

As of September 2015:

> Jordan Ashlee Jacobs is employed by Laborers Int'l. Union of North America 158 HCL.

> Jillian Rochelle Jacobs is Hospital Operations Coordinator for United Health Services.

> Emily Madison Ball is in eighth grade at the Lower Dauphin Middle School.

> Olivia Emerson Ball is in fifth grade at Conewago Elementary School.

Jo Ellen

Jo Ellen began her professional career with the Federal Bureau of Investigation (FBI) in Washington, DC, followed by a position with the National Security Agency (the top intelligence organization of the U.S. government), then the newest government agency—later to become the premium agency with the highest clearances required—where she quickly earned a high-level administrative position. She later joined her husband in his business, Lorenz and Lorenz Certified Public Accountants.

On September 6, 1958, in a double wedding ceremony shared with her sister Judith, Jo Ellen Thompson (b. November 6, 1938) married Eugene Kendall Lorenz (b. September 19, 1932), the son of Alma ("Bonnie") Corinne Miller and Eugene Hurdle Lorenz.

The children of Jo Ellen Thompson and Eugene Kendall Lorenz

> I. Janelle Corinne Lorenz Wright (b. January 2, 1969) (10th)

> II. Eugene Kendall Lorenz, Jr. (b. April 17, 1970; d. January 3, 2013) (10th)

10th generation (dates align with the 10th generation of the John Pifer Paternal Lineage)

Janelle Lorenz Wright manages real estate for her parents and her family. Previously, she was employed by KPMG Peat Marwick and as the private label buyer for Saks Fifth Avenue's catalog division.

Janelle Lorenz married Jay Oscar Wright (b. December 12, 1969, St. Johnsbury, Vermont) on October 25, 1997. They reside in Potomac, Maryland. They are the parents of

> I. Corinne Catherine Wright (b. May 29, 2001 in Sarasota, Florida) (11th)

> II. Theodore Piers Wright (b. September 30, 2002 in Silver Spring, Maryland) (11th)

11th generation (dates align with the 11th generation of the John Pifer Paternal Lineage)

As of September 2015:

> Corinne Catherine Wright is in the ninth grade at The Connelly School of the Holy Child, Potomac, Maryland.

> Theodore Piers Wright is in the sixth grade at Echelon Academy, Sandy Spring, Maryland.

Elizabeth Nan

Nan began her professional career with the National Security Agency in Washington, DC. She later moved to Southern California where she worked for the City of Anaheim. Following a return to Pennsylvania, she worked in Development for Dickinson College in Carlisle before finding her niche in Public Relations for Penn State's College of Medicine and Hershey Medical Center. Currently she manages and is the page designer for Yesteryear Publishing.

On August 18, 1965 **Elizabeth Nan Thompson** (b. August 19, 1942) married **Joel Keith Edmunds** (b. August 14, 1942), the son of Irvin C. and Jaclyn Beck Edmunds.

The children of Elizabeth Nan Thompson and Joel Keith Edmunds

    I. **Shayne Scott Edmunds** (b. December 9, 1965 in Northridge, California) (10th)

    II. **Jesse Joel Edmunds** (b. November 6, 1979 in Lucerne Valley, California) (10th)

10th generation (dates align with the 10th generation of the John Pifer Paternal Lineage)

Shayne Edmunds and his wife, **Grace Graybill,** are co-owners of the Neato Burrito restaurant chain located throughout South Central Pennsylvania.

Shayne Edmunds married **Ada Grace Graybill** (b. November 10, 1969) on June 15, 1999. They reside in Dillsburg, Pennsylvania and are the parents of

    I. **Aero Graham** (b. April 18, 2004 in Harrisburg, Pennsylvania) (11th)

    II. **Iris Isadora** (b. September 2, 2005 in Harrisburg, Pennsylvania) (11th)

Jesse Edmunds is an outdoor adventurer as well as an accomplished musician who currently performs in the Greater Harrisburg, Pennsylvania area. He resides in Hershey, Pennsylvania.

11th generation (dates align with the 11th generation of the John Pifer Paternal Lineage)
As of September 2015:

    Aero Graham is in the sixth grade at Northern Middle School in Dillsburg, Pennsylvania.

    Iris Isadora is in the fifth grade at Northern Elementary School in Dillsburg, Pennsylvania.

[i]   "Early History," *150th Anniversary, Curwensville, PA*, 1949, p. 11.

[ii]   Straw, Albert Y. *Some Genealogies and Family Records*, 1931: Press of Clearfield Republican.

[iii]   Charles Cecil Wall (June 21, 1903 – May 1, 1995) was an American self-taught historian and preservationist, who spent 40 years as Resident Director of George Washington's estate at Mount Vernon on the banks of the Potomac River, where he endeavored to keep the home and its surroundings in much the same state that it existed when the First President resided there. Cecil, the name by which he was best known, authored George Washington, Citizen-Soldier. As children Kay Thompson and cousin Bill Jackson visited Mount Vernon regularly. Cecil and Marguerite had two daughters (Mary Jane and Patty Ann) close in age to Kay and Bill.

[iv]   The newspaper account of this wedding was found in Bridal Greetings (1894), a book for brides and advice for newlyweds, a wedding gift from Benjamin Mosser (the pastor who performed the ceremony) to Elizabeth. This book is still in the possession of the family.

[v]   In 1948 Bill Jackson was legally adopted by Bradford B. Crunk, but retained (at Mr. Crunk's insistence) the name of his birth father "to always honor him," as Brad noted.

[vi]   Mother told us that this is the spelling Howard used and she continued with it.

[vii]   Howard used the "Jr." designation even though his middle name was not that of his father.

www.ingramcontent.com/pod-product-compliance
Lightning Source LLC
Chambersburg PA
CBHW041603260326
41914CB00011B/1376